Letting Go of Darkness

A Spiritual Path to Wellness

LOTTI GOODWIN

Letting Go of Darkness
A Spiritual Path to Wellness

Published by
Crystal Garden Press
PO Box 443
Arlington, WA 98223
Visit our website at www.CrystalGardenPress.com
Please see ordering information in the back.

Copyright © 2006 by Lotti Goodwin
All rights reserved. Printed and bound in the United States of America.
No part of this book may be used or reproduced or transmitted in any form or by any means, electronic or mechanical, including photocopying, recording, or by any information storage and retrieval systems, without written permission from the publisher except where permitted by law.

This book is intended for general information purposes only. Readers should always consult a holistic medical expert or their personal physician for specific applications to their individual conditions.

FIRST EDITION

Art Direction and Interior Design by Robert Lanphear
Cover Art by Anahata Joy Katkin
Photography by Lisa Cooper and Joseph Rossano

Library of Congress Cataloging-in-Publication Data
Lotti Goodwin
Letting go of darkness: a spiritual path to wellness/Lotti Goodwin
Library of Congress Control Number: 2005906769
ISBN 0-9771164-0-9
1. Self-help 2. Mind and Body 3. Spirituality
I. Title: Letting Go of Darkness. II. Title
10 9 8 7 6 5 4 3 2 1

Dedication

This book is dedicated to my husband,
Peter, whose humor and loving presence
have made my life as wonderful
as I always thought it could be.

Contents

What Is Life Saying to You? 1

Part 1: Our Multidimensional World

The Miraculous Human Being 9
The Alpha Spirit 12
Other Consciousness Streams 13
Angelic Beings 15
The Pleiadian Star People 19
Our Devic Friends 21

Part 2: Embracing the Mystery

The Personal Elements of Spirit 29
The Greater Reality 33
Awakening to the Light 36
Clearing Stagnation 39
Having and Being 43
The Transparent Ego 45
The Beginning of Chaos 47
The Rise of Fear 50
Waking from Sleep 52
The Work Begins 56
Entering the Stream 64
Losing Control 67
Avoiding Ambush 70

Relationships as Mirrors 73
Taking Flight 78
Pit Dwellers – The Ubiquitous Adversary 80

Part 3: The Unfolding of Spirit

Ghosts from the Past 89
Island Spirit 93
Meeting Melissa 96
Darkness Falls 103
A New Life Begins 108
Exploring the Darkness 112
Into the Fire 119
Coming to Terms 125
Holding On to Normal 132
Finding Her Light 137
Lifting the Veil 143
Home 151

Afterword 161
A Promise to the Day 163
Acknowledgments 165
Appendix: Fourth Step Guide 168
Bibliography: Selected and Recommended 171
Personal Pages 173

What Is Life Saying to You?

Consciousness expands, and the journey of life is a record of that process in the human experience. The contractions that push us into the physical world are echoes of a greater force that continues to exert its influence throughout life. But instead of birthing our bodies, this force births consciousness. It pushes us out of the dark and limited confines of personal mind into the limitless dimensions of light.

This book is for those on a journey of discovery into the inner dimensions of life, seeking the light they know intuitively is there. Many of us are in transition, our lives moving in directions we never imagined as we search for new ways of being, higher ways of expressing the spirit in us that ever seeks its freedom.

This book is also for those stuck in the mire of the past, frustrated that the health and happiness they want to enjoy seems always to elude them. One thing after another takes away time and energy until life happens so automatically that we've forgotten who we are.

The frustration that stalks us, despite our accomplishments, seems to derive from the world around us. But the world simply shows us what we can't see in ourselves; the distorted patterns that have grown in the energy field around our own bodies. Recognizing and healing these anomalies before they break down the physical body in exhaustion and disease is a part of spiritual care. Too often, however, it is a breakdown in the integrity of the body's systems that inspires us to discover our spirit's needs.

As long as we live in the vital eminence of youth, the patterns of negativity that bring darkness into the body can be readily thrown off. But increasing age diminishes our capacity for transcendence. We are compelled to encounter the unknown geography of our inner world and reclaim its abundance, or we become submerged in the agonizing realities conjured by our inherited patterns in our declining years.

Healing results from freeing our inner world from the past and bringing harmony to the aspects of personal spirit that compose our whole being; moving from an ego-based to a spirit-based life. The biggest job in moving toward spirit is dismantling the power of the ego. When we lose connection to the greater intelligence that guides us through life, we must depend on the ego to show us the way. But that was never the ego's role. In the beginning the ego supported our spiritual truth. But as we became unable to claim that truth, the ego stepped into the void and took us from our spirit's path.

How we handle our challenges in life reflects the progress we have made on our personal journeys. As we learn to work with spirit to enrich our physical realities, the answers we seek become more available and life more satisfying. When we recognize the ego's patterns that influence our lives, we are able to view our problems from a clearer perspective.

My primary focus when working with others is to help them cultivate a functional relationship with spirit. By integrating everyday experience with an understanding of the finer realms of reality, the success and abundance we can create is unlimited. Spirit becomes more tangible, more intimate. Ultimately, the spiritual world combines with your experience of the physical, and life reflects that harmony in the peace we enjoy.

The most common quality of those who are successful and content with life is the loving generosity they extend themselves and others. They have found their place in the world, and live in conscious gratitude and love. In this book I offer insights from my years as a counselor and energy worker that have helped many open the door to this kind of relationship with the world.

This approach to life allows consciousness to expand in its own organic way. Over time, as I did pattern discovery work with many different people, I realized that consciousness flows into our reality through different channels. Each stream has its own unique qualities. You may live with someone whose spiritual nature is incomprehensible to you because the consciousness stream their being reflects is different from yours. I describe several of these reality streams in Part One, according to my own interpretations of them. There are many more; some currently find expression in this world while others have already passed from it.

In Part Two we look at what human beings discover when they go inward. The inner world cannot be approached through the intellect; we arrive there by centering personal consciousness in the crucible of the heart. The treasures we discover on our journey make possible a new relationship to life. The power we gain from that journey has a different energy than we might expect. We are only beginning to move into a condition of consciousness that allows us to experience that power directly.

Ellen's story appears in Part Three to weave my observations into the tapestry of an individual's life. She moves through experience as many do, coping with the unpredictable elements of fortune, hoping at the end to find some kind of pleasure in the life she made.

When Ellen finally has achieved the security that was so important, events appear out of nowhere that threaten to undermine everything. How she meets those challenges opens her to spirit and the mysteries of the heart.

Ellen's story unfolds through her dreams and visions. The journey of transformation happens on the inner planes of life; in the outer world only the fulfillment awaits. Ellen's struggles are explored through their genesis in the world of shadows. Bringing light to that world by discovering the light in ourselves is the work each of us must eventually embrace. By learning to feel and care for the spirit that lives within us, we learn how to love, which is the point of a well-lived life.

It's important for people to be able to reach beyond themselves, to explore areas of reality not yet considered by their everyday mind. Even though the ideas presented in this book are purely from my own perception and experience, my desire is that they will inspire others to think about what their reality could look like if they were to chance moving beyond the safety of the known, closer to the heart of their own life.

June, 2005
Four Corners Farm
Western Washington

That which gives me life is the same that gives life to you. In that one essential way we are not different.

PART ONE

Our Multidimensional World

The Miraculous Human Being

*I am particularly fond of the little groves of oak trees.
I love to look at them, because they endure the
wintry storm and the summer's heat,
and—not unlike ourselves—seem to flourish by them.*
—Sitting Bull

Human beings have an energy signature which distinguishes us from all the other beings of light that share the world with us. It is an inborn quality, most pure in children. It usually fades from experience as we age, becoming buried under the piles of baggage we collect along the way. I have encountered only a few people who carry the pure energy of human spirit into adulthood. They have avoided becoming lost to themselves while securing a place in this world.

I know these individuals as powerful, reverent, loving men and women, well grounded in life. They often choose more difficult paths, knowing they will be guided and supported by many unseen allies. Even when they are burdened with hardship, they remain true to the energy signature of the divine child that defines their true nature: a communion of unwavering joy, perfect faith, and deepest wisdom.

This unique and beautiful soul signature is delight personified. Through it we live in perfect balance with universal intelligence, naturally connected to the divine aspect of life, both individually and universally. When we live in the center of these life-affirming energies, wholeness is not lost to the division of life between ego and spirit. Growth is channeled through immediate experience, not mired in the struggles that defined our past. When difficulties arise, they are met with optimism, ingenuity, integrity, and perseverance. Failure does not exist, only the desire to succeed through further effort.

As we each discover our true potential, this relationship with life will become the norm. Humankind is beginning to see through the rigid ego forms that shape our family histories. We are discovering the truth that arises when we become free of the lies that have blinded us for so long. We are finding our natural connection to joy. As we consciously create experiences that celebrate our unique individuality, we will grow without the need for struggle, and without the need for suffering.

It is a great thing to be human. Oddly, when I talk to groups of people about the various channels of consciousness that come together in our world, the last thing most of them want to be is the human one: they see no glory there. But there is glory and honor in being human, when one considers the tremendous resources of love and intelligence that are continually focused on our success.

We are like beloved children to the many great beings who guide us through this world. They look upon us with pride, and we should see ourselves with the same compassion and acceptance as they. The resources of the everyday mind remain limited until it is merged with the living intelligence that pervades the life of the spiritually awakened person. As we continue to overcome the limitations that narrow our perception of what is possible, those great beings that serve our growth will journey with us.

Higher intelligence communicates its presence through dreams, visions, synchronicities, and revelation, among many other avenues. This intelligence can be utilized to solve problems and prepare opportunities that the everyday mind could never formulate on its own. We might assume that the radiant intelligence which supports our universe does not care what happens to each of us personally, but it does just that. This becomes more apparent as we cultivate a direct relationship with the spiritual world and make it an integral part of everyday life.

※

The Alpha Spirit

The spiritual world is an extension of the reality we live in every day; it is inside of this reality. We all have access to this world and move through various regions or dimensions of it at will. The body that we use to travel through the dimensions of spirit inhabits the same energy field as the physical body. The spiritual body lives its own life, very often completely separate from our everyday perception. Its activities in the spirit world can be relevant to the tasks we carry out in this world, or they may not. The gifts of perception granted to the spiritual body are far greater than those we enjoy at the physical level. Its senses are global; for instance, sight is not limited to the eyes. It may be pitch black to our physical eyes, but our spirit's body sees as if there was light, and in all directions at once.

A Spiritual Path to Wellness

The spirit in whose mystery art was submerged was an earthly spirit, which the medieval alchemists had called Mercurius.
—Aniela Jaffé

I often call this potent aspect of spiritual reality the Alpha Spirit. It generates the life force that drives us to grow and expand. The vitality it supplies is used to express what we become, either through our own volition or through the influence of others. The Alpha Spirit holds the pattern for physical development, from the womb to the end of life. Its natural power permeates all we do. It is our most valuable resource in this realm, attending to the intricacies of our existence in the physical world. It draws to us the life-giving forces of nature, blending them with the nourishing rays of light that give us the power of transcendence.

Other Consciousness Streams

Many relationships we form in the spirit world are with beings we recognize as other than human. In those realms, we seem to know when we are talking to an Angel or a Faery. In this world, Angelic or Faery beings are likely to have the same form as human beings, and we would probably mistake them for humans. We can, however, recognize them by how they feel, by their particular energy signature.

Whether seen or unseen, these beings are here to help us move beyond the habits of darkness from which we have long suffered on our journey to wisdom. Great numbers of these beings from the higher planes attend our growth, usually invisible to our physical eyes. In the physical population, however, their numbers are more limited.

They know we are ready to see beyond the darkness that fills our lives. Increasing numbers of these beings are taking physical bodies to hold light in the collective field while we establish ourselves there. Both our personal and our collective fields are deluged with negative material on a daily basis, but with the help of the limitless beings who promote our growth, we will transcend this painful period. They have always been present to our progress, helping us create new advances in living and relating which increase our capacity to bring into being the kind of world we are so capable of having. Human consciousness is expanding everywhere, making everyday life a profoundly richer and deeper experience for the many millions of people all around the globe who are part of this massive shift in our collective reality.

※

Angelic Beings

People with Angelic consciousness are liberally sprinkled throughout the earth's population. They are powerhouses of strength and happiness, placed among us to radiate living light into the physical reality of human perception. Their light ensures that we will always find a way to move ahead, regardless of the difficulties that assail us.

Stabilizing human consciousness in the light of love is the biggest challenge we face at this time. Angelic light protects us as we let go of the old mind structures that block our way to spirit. The body's reality shifts dramatically when patterns are dissolving, and the Angelic presence holds us steady.

Angelics have lived among us in physical bodies, keeping their beautiful light alive in the human heart and mind, for as long as we have been traveling this path. Their energy fields swirl with sparkling showers of golden and silver light. If you can't see the magic in their auras, you can tell them by their awesome and loving strength, which is unfailing.

Almost always, they have what I call "fluffy" bodies. In the physical world both men and women Angelics often have a large and charismatic presence. They are fun loving and jovial, committed unreservedly to the happiness and growth of all beings. They love being together in small groups or large. Enjoying the bounty of life is second nature to them, as is sharing that bounty with others. They are joyfully generous in all things, having no ambition to accumulate money or power for the sake of it. They live naturally at the creative center of life, where they receive all things in abundance.

Being Angelic, they cannot contract and harden their energy field as humans are so capable of doing. If they could, the light of truth they radiate into our human world would be extinguished. Since they are unable to harden their energy fields, they feel all the suffering and chaos they encounter in life; they can't separate themselves from anything happening around them. It is very difficult for them to establish boundaries, or even really understand the concept.

Angelics can take on the patterns of the human world, but they never become comfortable in those cramped identities. The nature of their being is too large and joyful to fit into a human mold. Between the ill-fitting patterns and their inability to develop an emotional skin, Angelic people can suffer the worst kind of living hell.

They were created in wholeness, though, and the strength of that wholeness is their salvation in the physical world. If it weren't for the tremendous strength that is their signature quality, they wouldn't be able to bear a physical sojourn in this world as it presently exists.

When in a physical form, Angelics often feel the need to hide their strength and wisdom; they try to fit into the human dynamic. Angelic strength is awesome, and many humans are afraid of it, though they needn't be. Angelics are the most compassionate of beings.

Although they greatly love humanity, they do not understand us well, which may be why humans are sometimes so fearful of them. Angelics can become very frustrated and impatient with us, wondering why we don't ever seem to get it. The reason for their frustration is that they don't understand the human process of growth. They are aware that we are moving toward wholeness, but they don't know what it entails, since they were created whole in the beginning.

Angelics who are willing to live a lifetime in a physical body do so at an incredible sacrifice. Very often they are here for the sake of a human in their care. There are many Angelics who take physical form to insure the safe passage of their human charge through a particularly challenging lifetime.

Legions of Angelic support are available to readily answer any requests made by those Angelics who have taken on physical form, and so it appears that they receive what they need or want quite easily. Human beings, on the other hand, are here to understand freedom, independence, and responsibility. The Angelic host will interfere with human free will only in rare instances.

Angelics in physical form should enjoy themselves as much as possible, as this allows the greatest abundance of light to flow from them into our world. When they come to know and revel in the radiance they shine into our lives, and live from the righteousness and strength that is always present in their nature, they are amazing people to behold. They are true messengers of joy and peace, fulfilling their mission in this world by illuminating our dark places with their divine light.

Throughout the long passage of time, there have been many human-stream people who have worked through Angelic consciousness to complete themselves. These individuals devote themselves to preserving the spiritual integrity of those passing from this world. I call them Light Guides. They shepherd us through the healing period that follows physical life. In this world they often work in healing professions, exemplifying the same devotion to spirit that the unseen Angelics bring to us.

The Pleiadian Star People

Beings who live in this world through the Pleiadian consciousness stream have long since mastered the path of human endeavor. They have already faced and overcome the challenges to growth we face now. Pleiadians see us as their younger brothers and sisters. At each stage of readiness, they have been here to show us the next step, exemplifying our cherished ideals of beauty, truth, and freedom. They work among us as architects, teachers, healers, or musicians, any path that allows them to show us how to take what we have accomplished to a higher level of expression. They are civilization builders.

I have noticed a great increase in numbers of those Pleiadians who, unseen, enter the personal environments of those struggling to improve their own lives and the lives of others. These Pleiadians help us rectify the patterns for the future that we are creating around us. The confusion and stagnation of old survival patterns are rendered powerless by the Pleiadians' intercession, which allows us to move forward simply and powerfully.

When we encounter Pleiadians in physical bodies, they appear effortlessly graceful. They usually have a body type which is marked by a cool elegance. They use their exquisite intelligence to create flowing order and beauty wherever they go. When a problem develops, they immediately connect with universal intelligence, arriving effortlessly at the proper solution.

Their wills are clear and strong, making them masterful negotiators and mediators. A strong spiritual ethic marks their interactions with others, and they work very hard to stay centered in the light.

Pleiadians don't have the impatience with developing humans that Angelics typically do, being most often tolerant and compassionate in their interactions with others. They have been where we are, and they know it is just a phase, a matter of time, before we leave behind the darkness we have created, to walk into the light of true being.

Pleiadians may be recognized by the clarity of their energy fields. They are rarely found at large group events, as they need an abundance of very clear space around themselves and ample time alone to keep their creative energies vital and centered.

Typically, they are quite goal oriented and work hard to build the lives they want for themselves and those they love. From them we can learn how to have reverence for life, and how to create futures that provide comfort and beauty for all to enjoy.

When Pleiadians take on patterns early in life, they become acutely aware of the weight on their spirits. They feel sadness that the world has to be so, but they don't hesitate to do whatever possible to keep their inherited burdens from getting in the way of building a good life. They possess a fortitude that differs from Angelic strength in all its unmitigated power; rather, they possess an acute sensitivity that it is necessary to persevere, no matter what the cost.

Both Angelics and Pleiadians are faithful to the goal of success that humankind has set for itself. Both will travel this road with us until we have mastered life, however long it may take. We are fortunate to have their counsel and protection on our journey.

✷

Our Devic Friends

Numerous in the human population are the Devic beings who have chosen to live awhile in physical form.

They are, perhaps, the only true inhabitants of this world; all others see the earth as a training ground, a school. The Devics know the earth as their home, and they work always as guardians of the planet. When they come into the human world, it is to help us learn to be better stewards of the home we share with them. In so doing, we learn to give our own earth bodies the love and respect that will allow the indwelling spirit to grow toward its true purpose.

"Deva" is a Sanskrit word meaning body of light…
The devic level is the architectural dynamic within
nature that creates the blueprints for all form.
—Machaelle Small Wright

In Pan's world, the Devic beings take many forms. Their cultures derive from the geography and geology of the earth: there are people of the forest, people of the sea, the stone people, the people of the air, and the people of the desert. Every nook and cranny, every hollow or height, anywhere you might find yourself in the natural world, is the home of a Devic being well fitted to the energies of that place.

Nature is mysterious, capricious, and vital, as are the Devic people themselves. They carry the energy of Pan in their auras. It is a natural force that carries all the many voices of nature enfolded in its potent silence. When you encounter a Devic in the human world, you will be touching something essentially unknowable. Their natures run so deep that you would never be able to fathom the depths they possess unless you, also, were of the Devic world.

Even so, if you have some knowledge of the magical realms, you can often recognize the Devic ones who have chosen to appear in human form. Devics born of the earth element are durable and unceasingly industrious. Their creative energy is boundless and impacts the world in very practical ways. It's difficult for them to sit still. Their emotions can be very strong, often putting them at odds with others. You can easily sense a kind of impenetrability in their energy fields. They are certain of who they are, and that will be a continually fixed position.

Devics born of the air element are often curiously eccentric, but well loved for their sensitivity and inspirational gallivanting. Their social and communication skills are excellent. Emotionally, they can be quite neutral, or even distant. They have a strong capacity for empathy, however, which will keep them faithful to their commitments in relationship as long as the constraints on their personal freedom are not too stringent.

You may find it difficult to completely relax with them. Their powerful curiosity about everything and everyone is always at work, and the intensity of their inquiries and evaluations can be quite daunting.

Devics who arise from the fire element are dramatic and action oriented, being leaders and teachers of the highest order. Their influence is established by ruling the emotional environment through which they choose to operate. They do this easily and naturally, by means of inspiration and charisma. A fire Devic is a supreme agent of transformation in this world.

Those whose home is the water element are Devic people who serve the ongoing journey of spirit through the oceans of time we navigate on our way to wisdom. They flow with the mystery of life, wherever it may take them; for to them life is no mystery, nor is death. The water Devics are comforters for the lost and companions for the seeking. You can recognize them by the sense of peace they leave in their wake.

There are also those few from the human stream who have chosen to define their wholeness through the knowledge and wisdom of the Devic world. These are the Magic Users among us, who, even though they may have many loving relationships in their lives, still know they walk through the world alone.

The Devic's connection to life is absolute. Their powers of perception are highly developed, and they will know what is needed in any situation, as well as how to meet that need. They often work behind the scenes, unrecognized by others, moving life skillfully through time.

*Magic never disappears. It only finds new
shapes to inform us of its presence.*

PART TWO

Embracing the Mystery

The Personal Elements of Spirit

The fact that there is nothing but a spiritual world deprives us of hope and gives us certainty.
—Franz Kafka

I have been blessed to explore many facets of human experience intimately through the bodies, minds, and spirits of my clients. In my role as counselor, I combine talk therapy, guided imagery and visualization, pattern discovery, and energy reading to see the situation from various levels of perception. Each layer of information offers different insights, which together create understanding.

I believe that human spirituality is multi-dimensional. Our physical experience is permeated by a loving, incorruptible, and eternal intelligence that graces us with wisdom, love, and life. The personal elements of spirit that infuse the physical experience with meaning and purpose become known by their roles in relation to our growth.

In this book, I have described these spiritual elements through metaphor to make them easier to understand. Together, they may be experienced as our inner family. I used the designations that felt right to me as I helped clients recognize the facets of personal spirit in themselves that could promote happiness and well-being. I found the Heart Child and the Guardian of Wisdom to be more actively related to the life of the ego than the other members of the spiritual family, so our work was primarily with them.

Exploring the inner dimensions of being encourages us to distill the essence of personal truth from the flow of experience that constantly changes who we can be. As we develop a sense of self that remains solid and dependable, the flow of life that passes through us takes nothing, and leaves nothing. We remain who we fundamentally are.

Through the ages, the mystical disciplines of various cultures encouraged neophytes and seekers to find the keys to their own inner kingdoms. Through rite and ritual such seekers pursued the knowledge that would make them whole. Each culture had its own names to describe the personal elements of spirit that became known to those who sought them.

Use the ideas you'll find in the following pages to

guide your own process of discovery. Change what feels right to change. The important thing is to be true to your own path. Find in yourself that which is nourishing and alive, and carry it into your everyday life. Talk to your Heart Child. Give her a name—or him, if it's a boy. Give him a home. Make her life real. Acknowledge the miraculous presence of your Guardian of Wisdom. When you develop a rich inner life and ground it in the experience of the world around you, the miraculous becomes known.

As we discover our inner life, it becomes circular, encompassing the four directions and the four elements of nature, with the spark of eternal being at its center. This center is the home we make for ourselves, where peace can always be found. I visualize this land of light as a vast inner territory bounded on the North by a great, snow-clad mountain. A being of abundant strength and power, whom we might call our Guardian of Wisdom, lives on the mountain. God-like in its capabilities, this being accompanies us on our journey through lifetimes of learning, opening doors and clearing our way for progress, empowering us to transcend a difficult world.

The Guardian of Wisdom is aligned with the Heart Child who lives in the South, giving us visions which come from that sacred place. The child's visions show us a path to the life that was ours from the beginning, the life dearest to our heart. The Heart Child exemplifies the principle of growth that must find expression in the world. Its wild spirit embodies the essence of joyful discovery; it is personal spirit in its purest form, showing us the path to fulfillment.

Embarking on a path of personal change ultimately brings us face to face with the wild aspect of this eternal child. The first encounter always catches us by surprise—it is so vividly alive and joyful. After its wild beauty, we see all the things it has hidden for us, things that were dangerous to display; but even this offensive material is brightly and magically alive. The child's passion survives the erosion of time, being embedded in the original enthusiasm and joy that is so charming, compelling, and frightening all at the same time. "Is that who I was?" we think. We are astonished and delighted because we know it is.

At the same time, the ugliness the child carries is palpable. It is our ugliness, the ugliness we have believed ourselves to be. In a flash of comprehension, we know we can either embrace the child or turn away from ourselves yet again. If we choose love, the next time we encounter this eternal child of life we will feel the energy signature of the human-stream being in all its clarity and beauty. By choosing love we move closer to wholeness, of which the Heart Child is the creative center. It embodies the magic that lives in each of us, a forgotten treasure that can return us to life.

✯ The Greater Reality

Through our comprehension of love, we become whole and functional in the way human-stream beings are meant to be. The Heart Child brings joy and delight and a sense of the divine to the experience of being human. It connects us to the timeless present and all the magical potential this implies. When embraced with consciousness, the beloved Heart Child designs adventures that will bring our highest achievements in learning and growth. The Heart Child is heir to the gift of creative imagination which alone lights the way to one's true life. This creativity flourishes in the high frequency field of love of which the Heart Child seeks to be a part.

The intelligence of love is boundless and ecstatic. True intelligence cannot exist without the power of love to warm it, and true love cannot exist without a scintillating intelligence to guide it. These are the Mother and the

Father, the feminine and the masculine, ever creating the dance of life we are blessed to be part of.

The being that exemplifies perfect intelligence lives in the East, and is known as the Lady of Light. Through her bountiful nature, we can come to live in peace and harmony. The ideals of beauty and truth emanate from her presence; her feet mark the path to enlightenment. With gentle influence, she instructs our passage from knowledge to wisdom.

Her consort in the West is the Lord of Love. At the personal level, he holds safe the mystery that allows us to be and grow according to the design that was made for us. Even if we don't believe it ourselves, there's nothing we can mess up because all is secure in his keeping.

These two are in constant communion with one another, enjoying the beautiful views from the lush courtyard that connects the grounds of their splendid castles in the land of light. The Heart Child was born of their union, and finds comfort and joy in their presence.

When these elements of spiritual reality join in harmony, we come to possess the life that was meant to be ours. In the center of this wholeness, we know who we are. Living outside of our circle of light is but an unhappy alternative. As our inner family becomes more substantial, the outer world becomes more complete.

As we abide where all four spiritual elements converge, a spark of light—destined to become a sun—fills us with a wisdom that supersedes physical experience. In this healing place, our body's energy field aligns with the loving principles which are the matrix of an authentic life. We rest in the center of our own light, knowing it can never be lost.

When the body and spirit dwell in harmony, the Heart Child flourishes. The Lady of Light washes us with the wisdom of the cosmic Mother, and the Lord of Love strengthens us with the power of the heavenly Father. The two merge and become whole in an eternally perfect state. The Heart Child flourishes in the power of their union. The Guardian of Wisdom accompanies our journey through life, creating miracles we often don't even notice, but that open the way to growth and advancement.

The family and home we come to know in this way are established in the timeless eternity of the heart. This is the nourishing center from which we grow. This place and those who provide us a foundation are the essence of our spiritual character—who we become and how we express our truth are understood through the wisdom and support we find here. This is the world we create with our own light. Knowing this world makes our experience of the everyday world richer and more meaningful. Guided imagery, visualization, meditation, art, dedicating a journal to the circle of light experience—all these are ways to access the essential elements of our inner world and to grow through them.

Awakening to the Light

Transforming life from a battleground into a refuge is the core of this healing. It is possible to carry an awareness of the world that is ever golden. Even on the bloodiest battlefields or in the most stifling concrete jungles, that golden world is alive for us to touch. When the darkness parts and we see for a moment its golden promise, our faith is restored and strength returns, enabling us to continue the journey.

Being spiritually aware does not fix anything in the world, but it does make us available to energy that sustains a useful, joyful life. It gets us unstuck and puts us back in the flow where choice is possible, where we create what is beneficial. To this end, we discover spirit and let it work through our hands and feet and head to shape beauty in our life.

A Spiritual Path to Wellness

The Warrior of the Light is now waking from his dream. He thinks: "I do not know how to deal with this light that is making me grow." The light, however, does not disappear.
—Paulo Coelho

In a spirit-based life, we fearlessly ask for wisdom, inspiration, and intelligence. The mother who loves nurturing her family, the mechanic who loves repairing automobiles, the police officer who loves upholding the public good, the physician who loves healing her patients, the teacher who takes joy in his students' accomplishments—all these are forwarding the growth of consciousness in the world. These people follow the path of spirit. Spiritual integrity is second nature to them, and they encourage the growth of spirit in all those whose lives they touch.

Through adversity and chaos, we learn the art of balance and grace. As we overcome fear and turn to love, we rise to meet the golden promise set before us. Learning to trust our ability to use our spiritual intelligence is part of transformation. Trust comes up most poignantly when we begin to look at our old destructive patterns. We must become willing to accept what we have disowned in the past, and trust that we will be guided to the other side. With this hope, we begin moving toward a new life.

The present, which holds the fullness of life in its embrace, can be blocked from our experience because the past has gained a stranglehold on the body's vitality. We may want to do things differently, but the fact remains that the mental and emotional habits established in our body's energy field continue to bring us the life we have come to expect. Determining what these habits are allows us to free ourselves of them.

Information is everywhere because energy is everywhere. Anything you can touch or sense in any way translates its presence to you with information, not only of what it is but also where it's been, what has happened to it, everything you could want to know about it. Our bodies are surrounded by a field of energy, and a stream of energy flows through us as well. We are loaded with information about ourselves.

We live in a sea of loving intelligence which provides us with energy and information of the highest order. In essence, we are that loving intelligence. When we let our energy field stagnate and decline, the information it carries deteriorates as well. A static energy field encourages the presence of negative patterns. Because the body depends on the information in a healthy energy field to remain well, we decline physically as we allow our energy field to deteriorate.

Negative patterns create dis-ease at the spiritual, mental, and emotional levels long before they generate disease in the physical body. For this reason, personal transformation is most effective when it is consciously grounded in the experience of the body. All other levels of experience are engaged through the physical and recorded there. Everything we have brought to this moment of life is available as information in the energy field of the body. The construction of the physical body makes it a perfect conduit for experience by the consciousness that lives through it. We give continuity and relevance to the transformational experience when we engage the wisdom of the body to define obstacles to our well-being.

※

Clearing Stagnation

We hold patterns in our body that can be either positive or negative in their influence over us. The patterns that destroy our well-being are negative. Negative patterns occupy physical space in the energy field, sometimes completely overtaking it. A negative pattern is composed of stagnant energy that has degraded from a state of healthy vitality. Depending on life circumstances, the decaying energy will be somewhere on the spectrum from hard and brittle to thin and wavering.

The original, vital flow of spirit is distorted when negative patterns go unchallenged. These patterns eventually assume an existence of their own, becoming the background against which an incomplete life plays itself out. The beliefs upon which our negative patterns are based, if allowed to persist, define a path of struggle pursued by our rejected self, which over and over again tries to prove its worthiness. The qualities of true spirit remain undiscovered, forgotten in the shadows.

Negative patterns easily override conscious intent. Rooted as they are in the mental, emotional, and physical levels of life, negative patterns are a constant weight on the spirit; they even communicate their own ruinous agendas to the world at large. As these patterns find connection with one another in the body, the ego and its ghost are formed, which takes us even farther from the path our heart would wish to walk.

Eventually the stagnation in our body and mind will become intolerable, potentially compelling us to action.

A Spiritual Path to Wellness

We can begin by removing the sludge, the decaying energy clinging to the body. An easy first step to healing is using hydrotherapy, taking baths or showers upon arriving home from work, upon waking in the morning, and after any time spent out in the public world. Water dissolves the sludge that gathers in the energy field. We are sludge magnets until we start the process of releasing the negative patterns that not only generate their own sludge but also draw it from others with whom we come into contact.

Hydrotherapy is particularly essential after pattern discovery begins. Consciously initiating change strongly activates stagnant patterns, and your energy field will be overloaded with sludge very quickly. If it isn't cleansed, the sludge will hang in your aura, eventually sinking back into your physical body where it becomes difficult to release.

Doing energy clearing for a seven-year-old child made it clear to me how thoroughly sludge can diminish our ability to function. He was normally a bright and energetic boy, but he had grown listless and withdrawn. Doctors found nothing wrong. During the session, his patterns were clearly present, activated by issues being worked out by his parents. As we flushed away the stagnation, brightness returned to his aura. His mind quickened to its usual sharpness, and playful enthusiasm returned to his voice.

Children shift out of their patterns very quickly if they are shown what to do, since endless repetition has not concentrated the content of the patterns. Children's natural aversion to sluggish energy in the body is still intact.

Regular body work is very effective at moving stagnant areas of energy out of the body. Massage and craniosacral work are particularly good remedies. Choose some kind of motion therapy to keep the process going on a daily basis, whether it be a simple ten minute walk or a full blown trek through the hills. Regularly releasing the body to the wild is worth five stars toward regaining balance and clarity that have been lost.

What lies behind us and what lies before us are tiny matters compared to what lies within us.

—Oliver Wendell Holmes

Being in nature excites our spirit and releases it for awhile from the requirements of the day. Moving through the world with no particular agenda prevents the patterns from having anything to latch on to. They may be set off by situations that pop up, but the point is, they are not driving you. They recede to the background, providing your spirit an opportunity to flush and revitalize itself.

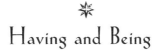

Having and Being

Every child comes into life to become strong and self-reliant. In a positive environment, the child grows in faith and courage. Ideally, we become the conscious expression of the gifts we have been given. Whether we discover those gifts in ourselves, and how fully we come to realize ourselves through them, determines our measure of happiness and satisfaction.

When life does not encourage development of self-respect and spiritual awareness, our gifts bear little fruit. In our culture it is customary to be trained in the value of *having*, without also being taught the value of *being*. Most of us are taught the same rules. If the individual is suited to those rules, there is success at the material level. To *have more* we must work harder, do better. Working harder and doing better sometimes gets us more. Sometimes it doesn't. Our culture is based on this one-sided dynamic. There is no *being* side to the coin. The spiritual aspect of life that could sustain and renew us is given little value.

Even as children we work hard to have what we need. But life can be capricious, and when *having* becomes *not having*, fear and anger are the common response. Fear pulls us into ourselves, and anger constricts the energy that supports physical and emotional wellbeing. Fear is used almost universally to control the behavior of others. Though sometimes it is present only subtly, it can limit and even destroy those under its influence.

One of the reasons we give little value to the practice of *being* is that it appears to require no work. In reality it is work, but of a different quality. The inspiration comes from within instead of being dictated from without. We do the work because we want to, rather than because we must. We can bring this distinction to any activity, no matter how original or repetitive the task, whether we do it for ourselves or for another.

The impact we have on the world and on ourselves differs in each case. When our spirit is strong, the work we do nourishes and encourages spirit in those we touch. If the energy of spirit is not strong in our bodies, we experience a curious flatness in our life. Work devoid of spirit is labor, and it is something we always resent doing.

As we clear the past from our bodies, spirit flows

in and timelessness removes us from the drudgeries of routine. Our lives are no longer bound to the industries of survival as our being becomes aligned with the sacred darkness from which everything arises and to which everything returns. Work becomes effortless, even inspired, as we enter into communion with spirit. Being and doing become indistinguishable one from the other.

The Transparent Ego

Clearing the past is mostly about returning the structure and function of the ego to a healthy and balanced state. In its truest form, the ego is a companion of the heart and an agent of spirit; it has no dominion of its own. Grounding our spiritual nature in the material world, it provides us a place from which to look out upon the vastness of creation. The ego gifts us with its ability to combine thought and feeling into an alchemical essence from which the beautiful mystery of experience arises.

The consciousness we enjoy as human beings is glorified by the ego's healthy presence. It is the mantle of sacred nobility we wear throughout this life, woven from the unquenchable qualities of strength and power founded in the Father, and the flow of divine intelligence emanating from the Mother. It was created to facilitate the growth that gives meaning to life.

When the ego is in alignment with our spiritual nature, it permeates our energy with joy, and good radiates from its presence. But when the patterns that inform it are contrary to the natural beauty we radiate as heart beings, our lives are marked by suffering as the ego is yoked to the necessities of survival.

The untaught ego is a fabrication of happenstance and folly that personifies the beliefs we were given about ourselves. It sets a course only toward that which sustains it. The pain that the ego protects us from also perpetuates its existence. When it was forced to become the protector of our spirit instead of its companion, the mutually nourishing bond they were meant to share was broken.

When the ego does not find a place in the spiritual family, it seeks its own path. Without connection to the higher agencies of life, it becomes stuck in a shallow mold of its own making. It can hold us hostage, and its hostile presence can take enormous stores of our vital energy to continue itself. When our vitality is siphoned off to meet the needs of the ego, everything that truly sustains us in life suffers: our health, our relationships, even our self-worth.

Fortunately, time allows us to undo the devastating effects of the compromised ego. When we begin the work of renewal, we can profoundly identify with the ego and the pain it holds. That the path to freedom should be over this same ground seems terrifying at first. Faith must carry us through that dark period, faith that something better can come as we reach for the peace and fulfillment we seek.

The Beginning of Chaos

Our solution to the childhood problem of survival was to invent a role that would somehow fit us to our family dynamic. To survive we were often compelled to focus our energies on meeting the needs and demands of those who provided for us. As we abandoned truth for the sake of safety and acceptance, we traversed a great chasm separating the world of spirit from the physical world.

We did this only gradually as we began using our energy field to hide the feelings we were afraid to share. As the emotional baggage piled up and became more controversial, we forced it deeper into our bodies. After a time, the places in our energy field where we hid things began to take on the qualities of the emotional energy we held there, and patterns started forming, like rocks that interrupt the flow of a stream.

Each pattern is a combination of thought and emotion bound into a physical matrix. The earliest patterns are fragments of the pain we felt as we moved away from wholeness. Each pattern holds the image of a child locked in a particular situation over which it had no control. The energy that gives these patterns substance is lost to us; it cannot be used for developing the creative potential in our lives.

Events that produced these patterns are tied to the physical cues that accompanied the event. Each time the event is repeated there are more things in the environment that become associated with the experience. In time we react to almost everything, the world having become a screen reflecting back to us all we have become fearful of. We become blind to the beauty that bore us here, so focused are we on all the things that have become troublesome.

The early patterns are chaotic in nature, with little or no thought content to give them structure, as they formed before our mental faculties were fully developed. Their eruption into the present causes confusion and breakdown of the order we have established around us. Their deeply emotional content makes it extremely difficult to detach from their influence; they feel so intimately real to us. When these patterns push into awareness, we feel in them a lifetime of betrayal and loss. These are the patterns that give substance to the ghost: the lost, rejected, hopeless pieces of our original self that serve no purpose in the outer life, it is the dark underside of the ego.

The ghost has a tone, or frequency. When it has grown heavy we can feel its dense presence within ourselves. It is our not-so-comfortable comfort zone. Our perceptions are calibrated to it. We mold the outcome of experience to remain connected to its habitual condition of dissatisfaction.

The patterns we take on to survive spiritually and psychologically, if not physically, are magnetic, and work through the natural laws that bind us to life. Our earliest patterns continue to attract and shape our experience, as long as we remain innocent of their presence and don't know how to reclaim the energy they drain from us.

The Rise of Fear

The child of invention—the child we all were in the beginning—learned to keep the life of the heart hidden and apart from the outer life that was fashioned more intentionally. The outer, more visible patterns of the ego are based primarily in thought rather than emotion. They are less vulnerable to chaos than the earlier patterns that marked our departure from the garden of life. The outer patterns provide relevance and mold the identity into what we must become. The ego manipulates the limited resources of its world to survive the life of isolation that it was created to endure. Its biggest fear is powerlessness, for its survival depends on appearing important and in control, even if only to itself.

Since the ego is a fabrication of our own making, it will personify the most workable elements of the knowledge we were given about ourselves. It will direct the course of experience only as far as this limited perspective will allow.

The individual spark of light attaches to the ego when it seems that this is its best hope for survival in the physical world, thereby leaving behind the guidance and nurture of those in the circle of light. When the light aligns with the ego its kingdom goes dark. The Heart Child is left to design life from whatever befalls it. It struggles to hold everything together for the light being that has lost a sense of its own strength and power. The Child is buffeted by the storms of an unkind world, trying to hold everything together for the lost light being.

The orphaned Heart Child seeks the comfort of family in the world it must encounter. The ego becomes its surrogate mother, a poor substitute for the luminous Lady who holds in trust the land that someday will be reclaimed. The dull and heavy ghost serves as Lord of the new household. The Heart Child's home is wherever the ego passes.

Over time, the light comes to depend entirely on the ego for its existence in the physical world. It willingly gives its radiance to the ego, which has no light of its own. As the ego becomes brighter and more powerful, the light forgets to let go and reclaim its independence. It would rather give its light to the ego and let it take care of life. Fear finally rules the light's experience: fear of letting go of the ego and finding its own way.

Letting Go of Darkness

When fear controls the life experience, self-care is abandoned in the struggle to cope. Therein lies the predicament. Only by consistent and deliberate self-care can we return to wholeness and the realization of our own potential.

What is needed, rather than running away or controlling or suppressing or any other resistance, is understanding fear; that means, watch it, learn about it, come directly into contact with it.

—Krishnamurti

The ego absorbs so much of the light's brilliance that soon the spark of light knows only a dimly lit cave and believes it to be the whole of creation. It forgets its own glory as physical life becomes ever more consuming. Until we again realize that glory, both within and without, the cave remains our only reality.

※

Waking from Sleep

Each of us possesses tremendous skill and power that often go undiscovered, buried beneath a lifetime of disadvantage and invisibility. Becoming alive to the potential within us is the beginning of enlightenment.

Acquiescing to the roles others have pressed upon our spirits nullifies the possibility of transformation and growth. It is only when we dismantle the patterns that bind us to the wheel of fate that we come into full possession of life's inherent meaning and value. Developing the capacity to know who we are and why we do what we do roots us firmly in the present.

Self-knowledge inspires consciousness, which in turn ignites and utilizes the potential of awareness. Awareness is the latent intelligence in all things. It lives not only in our own body but everywhere and in everything. The gift of consciousness allows us to plunge through the vibrant sea of awareness with abandon. There we can know the experience of abundant life and radiant peace.

Everyday life is the chrysalis in which we must find our wings. During the normal course of events, something happens that triggers a sequence of thoughts, emotions, and behaviors that are so habitual we don't think twice about them. If we can't see that what we're doing isn't the best response we're capable of, or if we recognize it but are afraid to change, the pattern will run its course, taking us farther from the life we want. We must become willing to see ourselves in the patterns we live by, see ourselves as others see us, and accept what we have always disowned in the past. Only this willingness to be with everything we have brought to this moment of our lives, the good and the bad, gives us a place to begin the process of renewal.

The decision to release your life from the negative potency of the past is a difficult one to make. It's easier to believe that changing something in the outer world will make everything different, letting you feel better about yourself. Initially this is true. After an outer change you might feel transformed, lighter, more lucid, but only because your patterns have been temporarily unplugged. They have not yet found the elements in the new environment that support them. Only conscious, intentional interaction with the new experience can ameliorate the otherwise automatic return to the status quo. If you carry the old pattern with you into the new experience without conscious knowledge of its influence in your life, it will automatically recreate the same conditions as before.

Life is always conspiring to bring us back to the path of spirit, but we tend to use the free will we were given to follow every path but the one that would bring us the most fulfillment. We can only come to the path of spirit through a decision arising from our own heart and mind.

When we start the work of dismantling the world our patterns have made for us, it is desirable to have the aid of someone who is knowledgeable about the process and compassionate with their approach. Those who seek this transformational experience are attempting to remove the irritants to spirit that influence their everyday minds in a negative way, and that create realities in which they are no longer comfortable.

As you consciously enter into your own transformational process, dreams become particularly useful to light the way. Dreams guide us. Beings whom we have forgotten in our circle of light—the Guardian of Wisdom and the Heart Child among them—speak to us through our dreams. When we have forgotten how to speak with them, dreams are the best way to benefit from their valuable assistance. Learning to access and interpret your dreams makes your journey a much deeper and richer experience. Taking a dream journal when you meet with the person who is helping to guide your process brings immense value to the exchange.

Developing your intuitive skills profoundly affects your connection to the process of transformation. These skills allow your process to be experienced directly by your everyday mind. Intuition allows you conscious access to the spiritual world. It is simply another channel for your senses to work in your life, profoundly expanding the quality of perception of which you are capable.

As you clear the sludge of the past from your body, your intuitive capabilities are automatically enhanced. When you notice these capabilities and employ them at the conscious level, you benefit from their presence. As we live simultaneously in many dimensions of the spirit as well as in the everyday world, it is very helpful to enhance our capacity to be conscious of ourselves and others, both those living now and those who have already passed. The ability to dream the future we want into the fabric of the life we have now requires intuitive capability. All areas of life can be expanded and enriched by developing this underused potential that exists in all of us.

❋

The Work Begins

Life can change radically once the work of transformation has begun. Those who make a conscious decision to embark on this path often believe they will remain in control of the process. One of my early teachers told our class the story of a man who had engaged his services, a very wealthy man who wanted to move his life to a new level. When too many things began changing and his comfort zone disappeared, this man asked my teacher to get things back where they were before, no matter what the cost. A million dollars wouldn't have been too much. But once the spirit is given the means to find its way to life, it will not go back to darkness. In the end the traveler's fears are unfounded. When our consciousness is attached to the ego, leaving it—letting go of that life—feels like dying, and in many ways it is a kind of death.

Dying to the old life is a process that can take as long as we need it to take. During that time the body is renewed along with the mind; outer circumstances shift around to accommodate the new spiritual component; relationships change to bring more inspiration and support to life. We give ourselves over to the energy of life, which is love, and the intelligence that flows with that love, in order to transform our being and our environment in the holistic context of time. In this process time is our friend. By its aegis we are restored and made whole.

The free-form approach to the process of transformation is not for everyone. Some people prefer more structure to keep them grounded in everyday life. The twelve-step approach is the most efficient way I know of negotiating this transformation. The principles of the Buddhist faith also offer a practical way of dealing with the process of transformation. Although most people could find a reason to join a twelve-step program of one kind or another, not many actually will. So, in a nutshell, I will paraphrase the principles of the program as I understand them, to get you started in a direction that has already worked for millions of people moving their lives toward enlightenment.

All the steps are about relaxing, letting go. The first step is about acceptance, simply realizing you don't have to be in charge or in control anymore. The second step is about having faith that you will find the help you need to be restored to health and wholeness. The third step is about surrender and trust, making a simple decision to turn your life and well-being over to a God of your own understanding.

This step stops a lot of people. The ego doesn't want to turn itself over to anything. But truly this step is only about making a *decision* to do this, not about actually doing it. Then there's the question of what God are we working with? A lot of people don't believe in God, partly because it's someone else's God they think they're expected to believe in. Too many people believe in a God that punishes and controls us. It's been suggested that you look through the *God Catalog* and pick out the qualities you would like your God to have, if you had one. Write down what you decide on, and that is the God of your understanding. If this doesn't appeal to you, then find somebody who appears to be doing better than you are, and ask him or her to be your mentor. Give them the position of your higher power while you're finding your way back to spirit.

The fourth step brings you to a point of honesty, simply admitting that you are a human being who is not perfect. In this step you dig into your mind and pull up everything you can ever remember that frightened or angered you. We write it down, which gets it out of the body and onto paper. Organize the material into four columns as explained below, filling each column entirely before moving to the next. This may take a day or two, sometimes even more. This list will show you what is blocking you from your spiritual life.

The first column is a list of the people and things you resent. In the second column, note what those people and things did to you. After doing the second column completely, the third column begins to turn the focus back on you, so you can see the ego's relationship to all the pain you are unearthing. In the third column you'll explain why you felt threatened. Was your self-esteem threatened, your material or emotional security, your sexual relations (either acceptable or not), or your ambitions? The completion of the third column takes you to the meat of the matter. The fourth column shows you your side of the situation, what you did. Honestly assessing how you reacted in the past shows you where change must begin. Were you selfish, dishonest, self-seeking, frightened, or inconsiderate? You can't get rid of your past, but by doing this step you rearrange things into the proper perspective. Your patterns shift and dissolve as you bring this material to the level of conscious understanding.

This fourth step is also about acknowledging and understanding your fears. To find the single fear that drives your life choices, make another list based on the fears you identified in the resentment list. Keep distilling down the fear list until it has resolved into a single issue. There are basically just a few great fears that most people end up with. The fear of death and the fear of looking bad are common denominators.

A Spiritual Path to Wellness

Step five is hard, but it's easy. After doing it, you'll feel like a new person. This step is about courage. You tell the God of your understanding, and another trusted person, about the mistakes you think you've made. You read them your entire fourth step list, as well as the list of your fears. This is an incredibly freeing act. It's an opportunity to clean up your side of the street of life.

We see in column four exactly what it is we need to work on in ourselves. When we can own our shortcomings, we can change them to more positive qualities. This proactive perspective really starts turning life around. If all our problems remain someone else's fault because we can't accept our own dishonesty or fear or selfishness, we can only be a victim. When the problem is somebody else's, *they* are the only ones who can do anything about it; only they have choice in the matter. Victims have no choice.

Getting out of yourself and trusting God and other people to help you right your shortcomings is a huge step toward bringing spiritual balance back into life. It is heartrendingly difficult to acknowledge your own dishonesty or selfishness or other faults, but it will heal your wounded heart.

Step six is simply about willingness, being entirely

willing and ready to have your life healed by a loving God. And then in step seven, humbly ask God to heal your life. Step eight is about forgiveness. Make a simple list of the people you've harmed, putting yourself at the top of the list, and become willing to make gentle amends to yourself and others. In step nine, you ask the people on your list how you can make things right. Do not ask this question of people who would suffer further injury from your approach, such as confessing to an already embattled spouse that you have been unfaithful.

This step should be done quietly and sincerely. It is not about punishing yourself or becoming a martyr. If the person you want to approach has already passed away, write them a letter. They will hear and respond. If you can't do something for them directly, do something for someone like them. The main purpose of this step is to get your life flowing again in the right direction by pulling out all the debris that's been thrown into it over the years.

In step ten you begin to take responsibility for how you live each day, using the first ten steps to clear obstacles to spirit as they occur. When you are wrong, promptly admit it and do what is necessary to make things right again. You discover how to do this by asking the person you have harmed what you can do to make things right. Keep your side of the street spotless, and put everything else in God's pile.

Now you are taking care of your own life, instead of everyone else's. You have created a ritual of care for yourself that is crucial for healing. My husband takes fifteen minutes before he goes to bed each night and writes in his journal about the day. The things that bother him pop right up. He can put them to rest before he goes to sleep. It's a simple way to keep the negatives in life from piling up. When I go to bed at night, I think of three people I'm glad I know. Sometimes it surprises me who shows up. In step ten, you take care of your own life and honor who you are.

Step eleven is about enjoying a conscious relationship with the God of your understanding through daily meditation and prayer. Through patience and understanding you grow in spiritual awareness, learning to be a better steward of life. Your relationship with spirit gives you the power to carry out this work. Step twelve is the result of doing the first eleven steps: you experience a spiritual awakening. For most people, this awakening is a gradual but steady process. For a few, it happens in a sudden flash of light. Either way, it awakens the qualities of charity and love in your heart, and makes it a simple matter to live these principles in all departments of life. An awakened spirit brings you again into communion with life, where you share with others the good you have found in your own experience.

Entering the Stream

The journey of transformation is a major component of human life. In its entirety, it is a process that takes us out of our normal reality into another that is profoundly richer and brighter with joy, love, and purpose. In that awakened state, we discover that we already are who we always thought we should be. The new energy we were looking for comes from that—inexplicably, just that. We discover the wonderful freedom of being empowered from our own center. Finding this beauty in ourselves allows us to recognize and honor it in others.

Each body tells a different story. The story that exists in the patterns that hinder us can be read as one might read a book, but the material presents itself to our senses through holograms rather than in characters on a flat surface. These patterns can be read by those who are trained to do so, an art developed in the medical practices of the ancient Polynesians. Each of us can also develop this skill to help us on our own individual journeys.

At some point, life expects us to undertake this journey. No matter how this time arrives in our lives, we can depend on certain things being the same for us as they have been for each person that has ever been transformed by this rebirth into life. Just as a caterpillar must become a butterfly, so must we find in ourselves the wings of spirit.

The first thing we can count on is that divine intelligence always guides the journey, even though our fear often convinces us differently. Once we've taken that first step, delivering ourselves over to the process of change, personal will aligns with divine intelligence to guide us. Of necessity, the life we knew must pass from our knowing. The faith that we hold to during this time of descent into the darkness of our most base patterns is the light that will accompany us to the other side. There it becomes established in our hearts as the essence of who we are, throughout eternity.

There is a deep understanding that the darkness we pass through is of our own making. In the depths of it, when our minds are numb to all else but just remaining alive, we are, even then, remotely aware of the power that accompanies us through our struggles. We realize, after we have reached the other side, that we were never alone.

Another universal element of this experience is the greatly expanded sensitivity with which we come to experience life. As we learn about our patterns and become more able to detach from them, the things that used to drive us crazy become bridges to understanding. We become more open to recognizing the patterns that inform our lives. It also becomes easier to see the patterns that engage others so automatically. When we are drawn into someone else's drama, we can look for the pattern that was triggered in us, instead of being dragged through a cycle of conflict that wastes our life. We can realize that our own patterns are the only ones we can do anything about.

When we experience a pattern for the first time, we are amazed that we never saw it before. Now we realize that this is something we have just let happen, despite being vaguely uncomfortable with it. The parent in the check-out line who blames and berates a young child for everything—including having given the parent a headache—hoping to look important and powerful to the captive audience in the store, is an example of how automatically our patterns relate us to life. If the parent were to become aware of this pattern operating while he was in the midst of its expression, he would be shocked. Our own patterns were formed by our attempts to protect ourselves against the patterns of those who attended us in childhood. Becoming aware of how completely your patterns distort your perception of the world around you is difficult because you are so involved in that distortion each second of your life.

Losing Control

Sometimes you don't plan to change; you don't make a decision to release yourself from the distortions that blind you to the sunshine of the spirit. Life just comes along and starts moving things around and making things happen, forcing you to stop what you've been doing. If you are thrown into the process by disease or accident, this becomes even more apparent.

The farther you wander from spirit, the harder life has to push you to come back. Often a person has no time to prepare for the transformation that will change their life, sometimes dramatically. Life gives us whatever experience we need to finally break through the formidable walls of the ego's defenses. As the walls begin to crumble, our vulnerability and fear become fully apparent. In the throes of that assault we may feel like different people, people we never wanted to be.

The almost instinctual response to this loss of control is to get the ego's world back together as quickly as possible, so things can feel normal again. When the ego patterns disintegrate in this manner, life takes on a surreal quality. The apparent lack of reality that accompanies this breakdown can feel unbearable.

Instead of giving in to the impulse to reconnect with the people and situations that would make life normal again, you do have the option of choosing simply to be present with what is flooding up from the depths, to experience the pain and embrace its presence. It will tell you what you need to know, showing you how to understand it from a higher perspective so that you can finally put it to rest.

We are closest to the ghost's chaotic substance when our hold on life is weakened by adversity. This can be an opportunity to begin a conscious relationship with the spirit that brought us here. If we remember that the emotions we feel in those dark places are only stagnant fields of decaying energy, and that their presence is due to our own neglect, we begin to have compassion for ourselves in a way we couldn't before.

If we are thrown into the process of transformation instead of encountering it with intent and knowledge, it can feel like being on a sinking ship. Chaos and panic can overwhelm our ability to cope—but that is the point. The light which has clung to the ego for so long must realize the limitations of its dependence. As the patterns of the ego creak and groan against the storm of change besetting it, the light realizes its protections are dissolving, its craft disintegrating in the stormy waves that assault it. That which can never die fears its own death.

As the personal will inherent in the ego dissolves with its patterns, the light is indeed set adrift. At this juncture in the process, our energies disconnect from the world and come inward. Others notice the different way we feel to them, not entirely present to their reality, as the patterns connecting us to them in the old ways cease to be. And indeed we are not present to the outer reality that we have been known by. Our spirit is working on the inner planes, preparing a place in the world of light for us to come home to.

The light that has lost the conveyance and protection

afforded it by ego has no choice but to experience the depth and immensity of the great sea of life, in which it finds itself suddenly immersed. Having depended on the ego for so long to chart its course through experience, the light will not, at first, recognize that its power of choice has been restored. Until we remember how to be nourished by the love and light that we are coming home to, until we allow the intelligence of the divine to inform our choices, we will continue to feel lost without the structure of an ego to live through.

Avoiding Ambush

When we approach change, we must be mindful of the power the ego has over our choices. It puts up strong defenses against anything that threatens the reality it has constructed. It becomes an enemy, even though in the beginning it protected us. When affirming any new direction we desire to take, there is a way to give that instruction to ourselves without setting our ego against us. Maybe you have a desire to find a voice teacher, for example, but you haven't been able to accomplish it over time. Instead of declaring, "I *will* find a voice teacher," you can say instead, "I *can* find a voice teacher." The word *can* keeps the desire for a new direction under the ego's radar. *Will* is like a command or order, so much that, if the ego is not in agreement, it will be disregarded even though it may be an important part of the spirit's path in life.

Distilling the presence of spirit from the raw constitution of the ego is the most difficult process you can ever undertake. But the rewards of taking life back into your own hands and heart are so much greater than you could imagine that not to do it seems unthinkable.

When you are working to renew the quality of energy that supports your being, you must remember to be patient with yourself. The mental body can shift to a new perspective in an instant. All patterns are rooted in the mental body, which makes us think that once we understand a pattern intellectually, it should resolve itself immediately. Sometimes it happens in just that way. Some beliefs we have about reality are simply not that important to us, and we are willing to let them go if something better presents itself. But other beliefs have much deeper roots in our being and are much more resistant to change. Our ego patterns depend on these deeply rooted beliefs to hold reality together. If these deep beliefs are threatened, the ego's defenses rise to meet the challenge, and the attempt at a new life design is defeated.

As our healing journey takes us through the increasingly dense layers of substance that comprise our being, it will take ever more time to clear the stagnation that has collected there. The energies of the mental body can clear and heal almost instantaneously. The emotional body is of a heavier substance and for that reason, healing takes more time. The dysfunctional conditions reflected at the physical level take the longest to bring back into resonance with spirit. Through this understanding, we come into harmony with that presence beyond our conscious understanding which changes things toward the good. The body and the spirit heal in their own measures of time.

The desire to change begins with the Heart Child, which designs the experiences of life through which the light becomes conscious of itself and of love. As long as the light is attached to the ego through fear, it will resist following the Heart Child's path to wisdom. The struggle of the light to become free of fear and of the ego's dominance is the mythical story that is told in each of our lives as we undertake the perilous adventure leading us to wholeness.

Relationships as Mirrors

Relationships are perfect laboratories to discover patterns that continually play themselves out in our lives. The world of ego and the world of spirit are both plainly recognized in any relationship. When a relationship falls apart, we can stand in the midst of the devastation and discover the patterns in ourselves that led to this conclusion. Or we can blame the other person, and then go on to look for someone else to reflect back to us that which we can't see in ourselves. For our partners reflect back to us not only the beauty of our own spirit, but the distorted patterns of our ego, as well.

The decision to face what you have run from so many times in the past brings you squarely into the present moment, where you find everything that you are—both the healer and that which seeks to be healed. Only in this moment can these two facets of your being find their common ground, a place to surrender themselves to one another. Whatever you bring to this moment is blameless in the eyes of the light and love that give you life.

Before self-love can be born, we are drawn into

relationship with people who have the capacity to reflect back to us the qualities of our own spirit, qualities that inherently feel very good. We may feel beautiful to ourselves for small moments of time with a certain person, or the feeling may last for a prolonged period. The light in us, however, wants us to have this feeling all the time. If we haven't yet learned to believe in our own beauty and someone else finds us beautiful, suddenly we have permission to feel that beauty in ourselves.

Life feels right and good until the patterns of the ego come into ascendance again, as they must until we resolve the unfinished business in them. We stay in the relationship for those moments when our spirit feels loved. Those moments are worth the struggle that eventually settles into the experience. Rather than letting the residue of struggle sit in our bodies, instead of letting it reinforce the negative patterns that grow in our lives, we can engage in the fourth step, getting the debilitating resentments out on paper so we can learn something from them. It doesn't take long to discover the nature of the pattern that is blocking us from a satisfying relationship.

Write your partner's name in the first column: "I'm feeling resentful toward…" The cause of the resentment goes in the second column. He left me. She didn't do her share. He made me feel like crap most of the time. You'll realize that all of your complaints could apply to any partner you've ever had, which suggests that you are standing in the center of a pattern that has run your life for a very long time. The emotions you feel are particularly familiar, if most uncomfortable.

Column three tells you exactly how you are affected. Certainly your self-esteem is affected, as are your personal relationships, because you and your partner share many of the same friends. Emotional well-being is shredded. Sex is out the window. Ambitions for security have been dashed. Going out socially without a partner doesn't feel right. The break-up has turned life upside down. If you stopped here, it would be easy to blame everything on the other person. That's why you do the fourth column.

Ask yourself: What was I doing in the relationship that didn't contribute to its health or longevity? Where was I at fault? I depended on my partner for my personal happiness. I never told him/her how vulnerable I was. I always acted like I was in control. I was self-seeking, dishonest, frightened. I wanted life to be the way I wanted it. Selfish. Inconsiderate. Whom did I harm? Myself. My partner. How can I make it right? For myself, I can do my own personal work to remove the pattern of unworthiness that puts me in these situations. The feeling of crappiness is something I experience a lot. It's something I have to own, it comes from inside myself. But at the end of every relationship, I think it's the other person who made me feel this way. Even in the relationship I blame them for it. This is the information you need to pry apart the pattern that keeps you in suffering.

At the end of the book is a Fourth Step Guide to help you create change in any area of life that has become a problem. Make copies of it and keep them on hand.

The help of another person, a counselor or trusted friend, is employed in step five to bring the full content of the pattern up to conscious recognition and acceptance. In working with a pattern, it often helps to discover its name, the words that give it potency. In the above example the pattern has to do with worthiness, so put some phrases together until one of them rings true. Perhaps the thought that generates the feelings of unworthiness is simply "I am unworthy." Or "Nobody likes me." Or "I can't do anything right."

A particularly common belief we bring from early

life is "I'll never be as good (or beautiful or smart) as her (or him)," whatever the case may be. It could be a complex of people, a combination of parent and sibling that cemented the pattern to your being. It will only make you forever fearful of not getting the love and attention you need. Untangle it. Let your Heart Child show you whom you are envious of or angry at. Your partner in a relationship is always really someone else, someone you can't tell your truth to because it is too dangerous. This focus work could take a few minutes, or much longer. The degree of pain that has been repressed determines the resistance that must be broken through.

Find the words that give the pattern power, and let them pull you into the pattern's vortex where only the past survives. Become willing to accept what you have dragged with you into the relationship. Then let the words bring you back through the dark tunnel of unknowing into the present, where you can see and touch and feel what is real. Say the words until they don't own your life anymore, and they become just words; until you feel a pop, like a bubble gently bursting in your body, indicating that the content of the pattern has broken through into conscious awareness.

In this way you literally change your body's beliefs about life and about yourself. As you translate the old patterns, one by one, into the truth that exists in this moment, you are released from the terrible compression that suffocates your spirit. This compression exists at the center of whatever disease or discomfort follows you through life, and its discovery and dissolution comprise the foundation of healing and transformation that brings you to wholeness. We learn that we are only as sick as our secrets.

✹
Taking Flight

Whatever brings us to the moment where the compression in us dissolves and our spirit is finally released from fear, also brings us to the birth of a new life. No longer are we alienated, or unworthy of goodness in our relationships. These are things we come to know as surely as we know that day follows night. The moments of transformation we experience by realizing truth are, in fact, physical rearrangements of the energy that supports our personal reality. They happen through the immediacy of our own senses, that we may experience our own process as we are transformed by it.

Releasing your spirit from darkness aligns you with the expression of your highest potential. That beauty is so easy to see in those people who have made the transition from ego to spirit. Their presence is rich with the serenity and power that before was compressed by struggle. They appear to be different people, if it's been awhile since you met. It is, indeed, as if they've emerged from the cocoon into the magical life of the butterfly.

Accepting everything we are in each moment creates a bridge to spirit. At a subconscious level, our patterns are constantly communicating to the world whatever it is they're about. If your silent communication is that you are unworthy, that's what people will understand about you, no matter how hard you work to appear not unworthy. In this struggle, we only reinforce the patterns that make us so uncomfortable. Worthiness cannot be found in the struggle to appear not unworthy.

Letting go of the struggle and going fearlessly into the center of the pattern that defines your fear, calmly saying the words that hold it in place—this gives your conscious mind access to the pattern. Once it becomes known to your higher mind, unworthiness becomes something that can be resolved, either through a finer understanding of the elements leading to that conclusion, or through actions that can lead to a different interpretation of the self. You can then experience the true quality of worthiness. The energy drained from your spirit by the pattern is restored, creating a whole new platform from which to choose your next relationship. In this way you peel away the dross from your spirit, layer by layer, finally exposing a heart of great beauty and strength: *your* heart.

Pit Dwellers
The Ubiquitous Adversary

*The fishermen know that the sea is
dangerous and the storm terrible,
but they have never found these dangers sufficient reason
for remaining ashore.*
—Vincent van Gogh

In many ways, the development of our tremendously complex nervous system enhances our awareness of the spiritual dimensions that interpenetrate the physical world in which we live. But what of the realities that operate from dimensions that do not edify our existence here? Just as higher-consciousness beings exist to guide and enlighten us, there exist things that have the opposite effect on our well-being.

I call them pit dwellers. Their usual form is a rudimentary emotional body rooted in a negative reality that cannot sustain solid structure. I have encountered them a number of times hiding in the energy fields of clients. On fewer occasions I have unexpectedly come upon them in nature, once at the back of a cave where I was enjoying a hot spring that flowed from the cave's wall.

I had been there many times and knew the place well. It was early in the day and few people were there. A dam of rock and mortar across the mouth of the cave made the hot spring into a pool. I swam to the back of the cave and sat on a wooden plank secured to a rocky ledge, a little out of the water. Suddenly a presence surrounded my head and throat, cutting off my breath. I could feel the cold presence of hatred chill my spirit in that beautiful place. It was the dense awareness I sometimes encountered in human energy fields. Its distinct energy signature could not be mistaken.

When I was overcome by a strong sensation of snakes winding around and into my body, fear and repulsion catapulted me into action. I got out of the cave as fast as I could and settled into a pool of cool water near the entrance to calm down. Over the next half hour, I watched others go into the cave only to emerge again very quickly.

As the morning wore on, more people arrived and the sounds of their laughter danced across the mountain. Three newcomers, two children and an adult, entered the cave and splashed in the pool, laughing and talking. A shadow left the entrance and fled into the woods. One at a time, the pit dweller could arouse fear in those who went unsuspecting into the cave, but those who went together in joy were not susceptible to its influence.

This experience, and others, showed me that the pit dweller is something distinct from the human spirit, even through it can enter into the human energy field and dwell there. In classical and theological literature, I found parallels between pit dwellers and what the ancients referred to as demons, or the devil. Somehow, the old manuals tell us, our beautiful natural world got tangled up with the reality of these dark things. The natural world is alive with power, and the beings that possess it are part of the breath and beauty of this world; they are not of the darkness that exists in the pit dweller's domain.

Pit dwellers promote destruction by escalating the

negativity that people carry in their energy fields. Humans are capable of anger and resentment, but those emotions pale in comparison to the pure hatred and compulsion to destroy on which the pit dweller's nature thrives. When a pit dweller is present in the dark patterns of a human mind, evil of every kind is invented. The person who moves with the compulsion to act on those dark impulses is nothing more than a slave to what can only destroy him in the end.

In some inexplicable way, though, pit dwellers play a role in the development of human potential. They provide an impetus for us to grow in understanding and love of one another. At each turn, we meet their promotion of hate and destruction with something greater and stronger, something we must call forth to push back their dark presence in our world. In this way, human consciousness is strengthened, and we learn to hold firmly to the light that is our truth.

Pit dwellers have no power in and of themselves. The weak substance of their bodies cannot channel focused intent. They lack cohesive force; thus, they can only promote the fruits of hatred and destruction from the stronghold of a physical body and mind. Their influence is strongest in those individuals whose energy fields have been made vulnerable by fear. Their need to gather power to survive supercedes all other considerations in life. The more intelligent a host is, the more effectively the pit dweller can control others through the host's personality. Lacking a fine enough intellect to control others through finesse, the pit dweller will employ brute force and violence to establish its base authority.

At its simplest, survival entails destroying everything that doesn't promote or contribute to one's own life structures. The pit dweller's nature amplifies this agenda, severely undermining the growth of human potential. Under this dark influence, our resources and attention are continually funneled into a survival-related focus that encourages and supports the pit dwellers' presence in our world.

This influence will continue to stain human history as long as we continue to follow the path of fear that has been accepted by us. Humans, in essence, are naked sparks of light that come into the world protected by a robe of energy that holds the keys to our highest potential. Our energy field translates our spiritual qualities into the ability to find our true place in the larger scheme of things. It perpetuates the natural, inquisitive relationship to life with which all humans are born.

The path we have chosen to enlightenment up until now requires that we suffer the destruction of that beautiful garment, in order that we may recreate it with our own hands. In the process we transcend the fear of death that limits our understanding of the eternal nature of the light that we are. Pit dwellers are agents of change, but of a low order. Their deadening presence promotes in us the strength and wisdom to benefit from, rather than be frightened of or victimized by, change. Struggle is a great teacher; however, we are ready now to move on to a better way of incorporating change into our lives.

Pit dwellers find no purchase in an energy field that is fully connected to the present moment. Our natural state of flowing beauty leaves them nowhere to hide. When we cultivate happiness and peace, we drive them from our bodies and minds. The light that lives in a well-loved, spirit-filled body can celebrate the common purpose that binds us: growth toward the mastery and freedom that is our birthright.

We are the beginning of a beautiful world.

PART THREE

The Unfolding of Spirit

Ghosts from the Past

Every once in awhile the time arrives when I must gather life together and throw it as far as I can up into the air and watch it fall.

Enlightenment is forwarded in those moments of profound clarity when, by intention or chance, our sight turns inward, and we comprehend something about ourselves that was unknown before. The droning preoccupation with everyday life stops, and light pours through the crack that has opened in our mind. These are the doorways leading to the life of the spirit.

Ellen's story is a record of many such incidents. As she learned to integrate them into the fabric of her everyday reality, her spirit began to heal and her life began to blossom. In the beginning, she tolerated the movement of spirit through her life only as something that needed to be controlled. She didn't believe life would benefit her unless she forced it to. Transforming that perspective into one that supported peace and well-being taxed her faith and endurance to the limit.

Her story begins when she and Daniel were high school sweethearts. She was anxious for life to be different then, and it felt like Daniel could do that for her. That hope was postponed to a distant future, though, when Daniel accepted a scholarship to Stanford, an entirely different world than either of them had ever thought possible. She was devastated when his plane left the small airport in their Oklahoma town, despite the promises they made to wait for each other.

The abandonment she felt defied all reason. Within months she married the judge's son to pull herself out of the spiral of loneliness and depression that consumed her. That marriage ended in disaster not long after. She fled to Chicago, a city she remembered visiting when her mother took her there as a child, to try and pull herself out of the chaos. The distance from all her painful mistakes allowed her to steady herself, and after a decade of work and study she secured a promising position in a prestigious corporate high-rise in downtown Chicago.

Daniel never left the warm Pacific climate he so came to love. After Ellen wrote him of her sudden marriage, he ploughed through a dismal year of grieving, going on to finish his studies and build a life

A Spiritual Path to Wellness

he often imagined her sharing. His love of the ocean grew into a business, teaching others the joyful art of sailing. As his reputation grew, his clients often asked his help in locating crafts fitted to their liking. A highly successful brokerage business grew from that, bringing the yachting elite of the world to Daniel's San Diego offices.

One of those clients had a daughter, a beautiful Brazilian woman whom Daniel married. Through the years they had two sons. The marriage broke up, however, when Daniel took several years to recover from a serious auto accident; his business suffered as well. What had been a temporary return to her family's home became permanent for his wife, and his sons now lived with her in Brazil. A decade later, even though the boys were now young men, Daniel continued to maintain a residence on both continents to remain close to his sons.

Now in midlife, Ellen was back in her small Oklahoma town for the first time since she had fled so long ago. The occasion was her grandmother's funeral. She was just coming out of the flower shop when suddenly her heart stopped as she recognized Daniel coming toward her on the sidewalk. A grin already lit his face as he recognized her, as well. He looked surprisingly like he had twenty-eight years earlier when they'd been so much in love: he was still tall, now with streaks of silver highlighting his dark curls.

His words melted the years between them. "Ellen, is that you? My God! It's been so long."

"Daniel . . . I . . . I don't know what to say." Seeing him brought up all the confusion and fear she had felt those many years before. She was pulled backward into a reality she hadn't thought existed anymore, one she had worked very hard to erase from her life.

"That's OK," he said. "You don't have to say anything. Let's find a place to sit down and get over the shock together." He offered his arm, and she took it like they'd never been apart. That was the beginning of their romance with each other and with life. But that romance would take a while to fulfill itself. There was a great deal of unfinished business to attend to before they were free to truly share the life which they had been waiting so long to find.

Daniel was in town for his niece's wedding, and he rearranged his departure time to accompany Ellen back to Chicago. As carefully as Ellen had crafted her polished veneer to meet the requirements of her corporate environment, she was unprepared for the loss of control that incapacitated her mind in his presence. It made her ill at ease, and if their history together were not so compelling, she would have chosen to simply continue her life as before.

Island Spirit

I pick up the glittering pieces that settle around my feet and walk away, leaving the rest.

Ellen and Daniel fell into a routine of visiting each other once a month. She went to San Diego on alternate months, a city she had never considered a destination point for her life. But through the course of a year, she began to feel comfortable there. She reveled in the long sailing trips they took. Ironically, when she was in college, the sailing club she belonged to was her biggest joy. Weekends with her friends, careening over the endless expanse of Lake Michigan with the sails tight in the wind, delighted her in a way nothing else ever had.

She had lost that sense of adventure and freedom as the years of work piled up. The promotions she earned were rewards for the complete devotion she gave to her career. A very secure life grew around her efforts. Now the question of what she and Daniel would do with their life together was part of the picture. It was finally put on the table when he asked her to marry him. It was something she wanted with all her heart, but at the same time she feared it with every fiber of her being.

Without question, everything that brought her joy was with him in San Diego. But her own life was in Chicago; people knew and respected her there. Everything that made her real was there. Walking away from all she had built in her life was unthinkable. "I can't right now, but let me find a way to say yes," she told him.

A coworker, aware of Ellen's dilemma, brought her to a holistic clinic not far from their offices, and introduced her to a Hawaiian healer who was there on one of the periodic visits he made from the Islands. Ellen had several sessions with him before he returned to Hawaii, beginning a journey that would transform her being. The healer asked her to bring a dream to their first session. It was one she had just the night before.

She found herself in a hut watching two Asian women preparing food. Through the open door Ellen saw a freeway in the distance. Daniel was speeding past in a beautiful new car. She wanted to go with him but did not leave the hut. Two tubs filled with clear water flanked the doorway.

Ellen told the healer that she awoke from the dream with intense feelings of sadness and loss. She thought the dream was perhaps a sad reminder of when she had watched Daniel leave so long ago. "No," the healer said. "The dream is now." He went on to explain how the hut symbolized the spiritual and eternal aspect of her self, and the potential she had yet to realize. The presence of the Asian women preparing food was a message that transformation was, even now, occurring at a very deep level. They were combining the raw materials of her feminine nature into something transcendent. The tubs of water indicated the spiritual renewal that would foster a transcendent understanding of her self.

"The freeway shows the direction of your personal destiny," the healer said. "The car shows you want to follow that destiny with Daniel." He discussed the prominence of the number two in her dream. "You are someone who seeks union in love and companionship. It also means you can be easily overcome if you feel threatened by the loss of love. Perhaps this is your biggest fear."

Ellen recognized this in herself. The pain of loss all those years before still haunted her. Even though her spirit was reaching out for meaning and fulfillment, the past still claimed her, threatening to extinguish any future happiness she and Daniel might create. "Next session we will find the places in your body that keep you from claiming your spiritual path," the healer said. "We will start emptying them out."

Meeting Melissa

I carry them on a journey looking for new shapes to fit them to, a kaleidoscope puzzle that is me.

This healer came from a long line of medical kahuna on the big island of Hawaii, and was skillful in many applications of the science. Some in his family line had attended the great kings and queens of the land when it was a monarchy. He had combined a degree in medicine with the healing traditions of his ancestors to create a holistic approach to treating disease. He believed the health of the body depended on the health of the spirit. His healing hands were skilled at seeing and hearing the problems of the spirit through a deep sensing of the energetic elements in the patient's body. The spirit itself described to him the blocks to its wellness and the path of healing that would make it whole.

The ancient healers likened spiritual energy to water. If water becomes blocked and stagnant, it will not support healthy life. They saw that the same is true with the energy that flows through us. They were skilled at removing the blocks to health and happiness that inevitably arise in everyday life. They also taught their patients how to take personal responsibility for keeping their energy fields clear. This work is part of a benevolent system of treatment that creates harmony and stability at both personal and interpersonal levels, traits that have always been highly regarded in the Polynesian culture.

In Ellen's sessions with the Hawaiian healer, she became clear about the patterns that kept her engaged in struggle, and where they were situated in her body. She became connected to the reality of her spirit in a way she never had before. Spirit had always been a distant concept in her life, something given over to other powers in the world. This approach to bringing harmony to her life was satisfying, in the sense that she could develop solutions to her problems based on immediately relevant information.

Letting Go of Darkness

As the disparate fragments of Ellen's inner world were discovered one by one, she began the arduous task of understanding and accepting the broken pieces of spirit they embodied. One of the patterns she became familiar with lay inside her back, below her left shoulder. The physical aspect of the pattern was a sharp pain that often caught her by surprize. A heavy concentration of fear and worry rested there. The heavy energy carried within it a shadow of Ellen's Heart Child.

"She appears to be about six years old," the healer said. "She is expecting us to criticize her. She's very defiant and doesn't particularly want to talk to us. She is always prepared for the worst. What is she so afraid of?"

Ellen remembered the part of herself that felt those things, surprised it was coming up again. "She's afraid to fail, and she's afraid of being left alone," she replied.

"She says that being left alone means there will be no one to care for her. Is that what you believe?" he asked her.

"Of course it's not what I believe," Ellen defended herself. "I used to believe that, but I don't now."

"What is this child's name?" Ellen was surprised by the question.

"Melissa," she responded, a little too quickly she thought. Where did that name come from?

"So not being cared for is Melissa's biggest fear?" the healer asked.

"Yes," Ellen said, feeling the truth of it in her body's response.

Ellen continued to think about Melissa's reality after their session was over. "How does she help you most?" the healer had asked. Ellen couldn't answer at the time, but now she knew that Melissa protected her from judgment. Her responses to people were always calculated to keep them at a distance.

Melissa's sub-reality was further explored in Ellen's next meeting with the healer. "It seems that your deepest wish is to have people think well of you," he said. "But the pattern that Melissa expresses says that she will only look for the worst from people, and so that is what you will notice. Patterns are like magnets. They bring to our lives that which reinforces their reality.

"It's important to understand that Melissa can't be anything but defiant and confrontational," he went on, "not very good qualities to bring into your relationship with Daniel. If he comes with no judgment about you, Melissa doesn't know how to incorporate him into your life. She needs something to defend herself against, and with Daniel there may be nothing."

"Yes." Ellen was thoughtful for a moment. "That's what I always loved most about him. He completely accepted me no matter how I was."

"He is your Guardian Angel in this life," the healer said matter-of-factly. "Actually, he has no choice but to love and accept who you are." Laughter accompanied his assessment. "I see he has come into this life from the Angelic realms because you have chosen this lifetime to be one of incredible transformation. He can be closer to you in the form he has taken."

Ellen regarded his comments with humor. "So that's the glue that holds us together," she said.

"On a different note," the healer said, "I feel a tremendous tiredness through your whole energy field. All your patterns have been running in high gear this past year trying to fit Daniel into your old reality, with little success it seems. I would suggest that you check out this condition with your doctor, and find some ways to support your health during this transition. Your patterns will continue to drain your energy until your beliefs about yourself and about life begin shifting to a higher level of understanding. Then your patterns will begin to dissolve altogether."

"How can I start dissolving those patterns now?" Ellen asked.

"Let's go back to the pattern Melissa lives in," the healer suggested. "Feel the layers of emotion you encounter as she relates her experience to us. We have passed through the layer of fear and worry. Now she is showing us her grief and anger. What pictures do you see?"

"I see Keith," Ellen said. "I was married to him just out of high school. He was on my back about everything. There was no way to please him. We fought all the time." Ellen didn't appear angry, but the dense emotion boiled into the atmosphere around her body. The next layer held shame and more grief, forgotten by Ellen's everyday mind. Ellen used Melissa's angry energy to repel the judgment and criticism she anticipated at every turn, avoiding the shame that was the pattern's only other response to such charges, as well as the intense grief that others should condemn her in that way.

"We're coming to the root of this pattern now," the healer said. "Powerlessness is what holds everything else together. Grief lies with this layer as well. Let's see if we can get things moving." As he held his hands over the pattern in her back, Ellen felt a curious sensation. Everything in her became very plastic; each bone and organ became very distinct in her awareness, while a rich warmth saturated every particle of her being.

In the midst of that deep experience of herself,

Ellen recognized something she had long forgotten. It was the blissful sweetness of her Heart Child, though she didn't know what to call it. She just knew it was the essence of her self, and that all of life used to feel the way she felt now. The sudden shift in her body's reality brought her awake to a level of consciousness that had slipped away over the years.

"The part of you that knows the way to freedom is close by. Ask what we should call her," the healer said.

"Her name is Sage," Ellen responded.

"Sage is what is real inside of you," the healer said. "Remember that the shadow children, like Melissa, are just patterns, even though their anguish feels very real. They are here only to remind us of the truth we've forgotten. Sage crossed a great bridge of sorrow long ago to become Melissa. In doing so, she took on the mantle of darkness so that your spiritual survival would perhaps be possible. Now that you recognize her, she can help you find the answers you seek."

As the burden of a distant past filtered out of her body into the light of consciousness, Ellen said, "Sage is showing me the ocean. It's unbelievably beautiful, and it is close to my life; a different life than I have now. How do I let go of everything that's important to me here, to have that?"

"Feel the freedom you have in your body right now," the healer suggested. "Trust that. Don't pull the old patterns back so quickly. Once you're back in the world, they'll return soon enough. All we've done today is take them apart for awhile. You need your patterns until you get more comfortable with what your spirit is showing you. In a week or so you'll feel your patterns coming back together, but they won't be as heavy as before. Your spirit won't give them so much energy the next time. When you see a pattern coming up, do something other than what you normally would. There are no choices in your pattern reality. You must be the one to recognize that and take the power for living your life into your own hands, even though your patterns would deny you that power."

Darkness Falls

The child tugs impatiently at my heart. My spirit knows where it wants to be.

On her next visit to San Diego, Ellen went with a confidence and sense of belonging that had been missing before. Daniel embraced her new enthusiasm with an open heart. It seemed at last that their life together might actually become a reality. The weekend they had together was extended because of the Fourth of July holiday. They decided to get a suite at the old Coronado Hotel and watch the fireworks on the beach. After a long day of sun and surf, Ellen was so fatigued that they had dinner in their suite and watched the fireworks through the window.

The next morning she felt much better, and the idea of spending the day sailing greatly appealed to her. But by noon her body felt used up, entirely emptied of vitality. Daniel took her below and made her comfortable in their stateroom before turning the boat back toward shore. He was deeply concerned that something was seriously wrong. His mind was awash with childhood memories of his mother who had been so crippled by fatigue. He had helped care for her during her long illness, carrying meals cooked by his father up the stairs to the room where she always lay.

As soon as they landed Daniel took Ellen to the emergency room. She was given a bed and hooked up to IV fluids while other tests were done. A doctor appeared as soon as the lab completed the blood work. He pointed out the abnormalities on her slides. They were consistent with some types of cancer, and he wanted to keep her there to do more extensive testing. The rest of the holiday was spent in the hospital, where Daniel attended to the details of the situation with a skillful and loving hand.

Ellen's doctor reappeared on the second day to tell them she had leukemia, and that further testing would be required to determine its progress and a treatment plan for it. The diagnosis stunned her. In the back of her mind she was still waiting to live her real life. Now, suddenly, she might never experience the fulfillment of that desire. The moment she heard the diagnosis, she knew life was no longer about making deals. Whatever was going to happen would just happen.

She saw the disease as a kind of judgment that had caught up with her, even though Daniel tried to keep her focused on a positive frame of reference. Back in Chicago, after a month of testing, she knew the cancer was stage two and that she would need to have chemotherapy to treat it. She reluctantly arranged medical leave. Work was the center of her existence, and letting it go for such an extended period was the hardest thing she had ever done. The emotional roller coaster she'd been on for the past year finally stopped. Her struggle to control the way events would unfold in her life seemed no longer possible, or even relevant. The exhaustion that had dogged her for so long was finally consuming her.

In the months to come, Ellen's fight for life would be waged in the dark corridors of her heart as much as in the brightly lit rooms of technology and science. By holding Daniel dear in her life, she was defying a belief system that exacted a penalty for cultivating happiness for its own sake.

Daniel's gift to her was his acknowledgment of the light she had once known in herself. The light had been lost, and she hadn't even realized it until now. Ellen made a revolutionary decision in the fuzzy silence that permeated her shell-shocked mind to do whatever was required to find the life she was now so close to losing forever.

As the cancer took more and more of her energy, it became increasingly difficult to maintain an objective view of the chaos that now flowed unhindered to the surface of her mind. Ellen sank into a weariness that was incomprehensible to her. The old determination to shut out everything that didn't align with her immediate goals now became a futile conceit. In the dark days that followed, her consciousness became fused with the battered spirit that finally lay exposed in her body, and it felt curiously impotent and paralyzed. If Daniel hadn't insisted on staying with her during that first month of uncertainty, she would have called into being whatever defiance still left to her and marched into the experience alone, as she always had.

But during that month of transition, Daniel was her Guardian Angel in the truest sense. He kept copious records of each doctor's consultation. He researched her condition thoroughly, discussing his information with her doctors. He fielded her calls and kept unessential interaction at a distance. He wanted her only to feel peace and that she was loved.

The end of a long month of uncertainty was in sight as Daniel helped Ellen create a program of integrated treatment and care that would utilize a team of doctors and practitioners to stimulate healing in body, mind, and spirit. Six months of chemotherapy was only one of the elements that promised to put the disease in remission. Ellen's relief at finally having a plan in place was immense, as if a death sentence had been lifted. If she could know how to understand something, no matter how difficult or awful the thing might be, she could find a way to accept it into her life.

A New Life Begins

*I am compelled to follow,
trusting my heart to take me home.*

Once the groundwork was laid, Daniel returned for a time to his life in San Diego. While he was gone, Ellen found it comforting that he had filled the gaps for her while she was struggling to maintain her sanity. In his research he had come across a book called *The Macrobiotic Way*. It described a nutritional program based on seasonal, organic vegetables, steamed and eaten with brown rice, that encouraged the body's healing response. It was a dramatic departure from her usual diet, which was heavy on refined and processed foods. They started eating the new foods together, and this made it easier to enjoy the change.

A new juicer sat on Ellen's kitchen counter. She had stuck with apples, carrots, and bits of ginger in the beginning, but now she was experimenting with beets and kale. She was encouraged when her fatigue began to diminish. Her body welcomed the new foods, and she began to feel lighter than she had in a long time. As she modified her eating habits to support her goal of health, she noticed a growing peace in her body as the food-related stress she had ignored began dissipating from her digestive tract. Her naturopath devised a supplement plan to support her failed immune system through the coming months of treatment.

Daniel planned to come from San Diego for her first round of chemotherapy. Ellen would spend one week each month in an infusion room, an hour each day. Then there would be three weeks to recuperate after each week of treatment. After six months she would be finished. They spoke every day on the phone, planning how they would celebrate when she was done. The long-distance relationship that never happened after high school was now a cherished part of her life; it was as if she were finally catching up on something she had missed.

Ellen's days became bittersweet as her past began falling away from the present. At the same time that she saw Daniel's commitment to her strengthen, she struggled against the powerlessness she felt in the face of a disease that was destroying all the defenses she had so carefully built against her own pain. Encouraged by the guidance of a counselor, she brought her pain to life on the pages of a journal she titled "Cancer Journey." The dispossessed children who had long lived in the shadows of her inner world came out to meet her.

In those forgotten reaches of Ellen's inner world, time had torn and twisted the shredded fragments of her heart's life into fantastic shapes of anger and fear. She no longer possessed the energy to keep them down. Finally free, they erupted to the surface of her mind. With pen and ink, Ellen identified the phantoms that held ransom her waning vitality. A lumpy, sunless figure appeared on the page before her. Grimy from work, the figure was a little girl, even though she appeared to be essentially sexless. Ellen then drew another little girl wearing a pretty dress and shiny shoes to stand beside the first child. But the beautiful child was listless and weak.

As she considered the two images, Ellen was inspired to draw a stroller that would hold both girls. She knew the grimy one couldn't enjoy riding in the stroller because work was important to her. Ellen wanted to give her something to do that wouldn't be tedious, so she gave her the job of watching over the beautiful child. She drew a blanket on the grass near the stroller so the girl could lie down when she got tired and take a nap.

In Ellen's reverie the lumpy child took a nap while

the beautiful child became an infant again. The infant sucked continually at nothing, its blank eyes fastened on some inward need that seemed to consume its whole being. A breast appeared and the child was given a golden elixir from it, bringing contentment to her body. Ellen was surprised at the neediness of the beautiful child and the compulsion that drove the other. She recognized the compulsive drive that had dominated her life until now, in which she had even taken pride. But the neediness was less obvious to her. The emptiness of the child frightened her. She wasn't ready to see herself in that light.

Ellen's strong ability to successfully oversee the details of her life had long compensated her for not having the magic of love, the golden elixir of life, to sustain her, to bring contentment to her body. The trade-off had never been of consequence; it was just how life was. She could see that the grimy child obviously needed care and rest, but the other child's need for nurturing and love was something Ellen was not ready to understand yet. After all, she had made her life perfect. The nurturing and love should just be there. So she did the only thing she could: she pushed the material back into the realm of blind unknowing that takes so much energy to sustain. She saw what she could allow herself to see and worked with that. Speaking only to the distress of the first child, she wrote on the sketch, "Because I'm such a mess, no one will love me enough to take care of me."

To dissolve that belief, she wrote simply, "Thank you, Angels, for giving me rest," as if it was something she already possessed. With attention, Ellen's newly inspired viewpoints could combine to bring about an important shift in consciousness. The creation of her new reality would unfold one step at a time, one day at a time, one motion at a time, one thought at a time.

✻

Exploring the Darkness

We travel until I've almost given up. At last we're here, on a crystalline hillside, the sun pouring down its incredible rays.

Investigating the beliefs she held about herself and her life was a wholly new experience. After learning she had cancer, Ellen realized that the beliefs which had sustained her up to this point could not sustain her over the long haul. The persona she had cultivated to make life work could exist only as long as she could suppress those parts of herself which she was so fearful of exposing.

She kept going back to the pages of her journal to make known those fearful images to herself. The page she had titled Tyrannized Child was particularly compelling. The creation of this figure with no arms, hunched over on the ground, had been an extremely painful exercise. She had worked on the page as if she were a child again, scribbling in the margins about what made the child so full of fear and discouragement. Its only desire was to go away and hide. The figure was unfamiliar to her conscious mind, but it had power to draw from her things that had long been hidden.

Ellen read the words surrounding the figure over and over again, sometimes aloud. Finally she felt a pop, like a bubble bursting in her mind. Her body let go of something she hadn't known was there. Sounds from outside the window entered her awareness again. When she looked at the page now, it was just a drawing with some words around it. The images didn't suck her into another world filled with chaos and pain. She felt compassion and sadness for the part of her spirit that had lived so long in such a miserable condition.

As the dangerous emotions of the tyrannized child

came to the surface of Ellen's mind, she was able to recognize the shadow thought that had cemented those emotions to her: "I'll never be good enough to have what I need." It suddenly occurred to her how all her shadow children depended on others to give them the acknowledgement, care, and love they needed. When that care was not forthcoming, the shadow children acquiesced to their fate and became reflections of it. She had yet to realize her autonomy in relation to the shadow children, which defined her feelings about her self. She had yet to realize that the light that carried her into existence was herself, and that it had the power to choose from the infinite possibilities offered in life those things that would bring her satisfaction and peace.

Several days before Daniel was to come for her first round of treatments, Ellen had a dream that set a choice before her. She was part of a great formation of soldiers marching down a wide road. Suddenly the soldiers stopped to allow a birth to take place in the midst of the regiments. Two perfect beings, a man and a woman, emerged from separate earthen vessels. The pair seemed like gods coming into the world, extraordinarily beautiful, in the prime of life. Ellen's attention was particularly fixed on the female, arching out of her birthing vessel, a broad smile on her face, radiance pouring from her. The man and woman stood together, and a glorious wedding celebration ensued.

Ellen dreamed of the woman again later that night. In the second dream, the woman purposely folded her graceful form into an earthen cell. Peaceful awareness marked her countenance as she disappeared into it. Then, for the second time, she emerged from the darkness of organic confinement and stood tall and free in the glowing light of her own beauty. Ellen felt the warmth and love of her words: "You can learn and grow only by experience. Until now your experience has been defined by your patterns. They limited your reality, forcing you to endure hopeless isolation. But your determination to move forward has brought you to this place in your life. You can choose freedom, or you can spend life in the limitations you have created. He and I manifest your perfect expression. Choose what is true for you, Ellen, and you will find the way to us, and to your real life."

Ellen meditated on her dreams for several days. She understood their meaning. It was true she had lived a regimented existence, but her desire had always been to engage the world creatively, to break out of the restrictions in her life.

She worked with her therapist to understand the

journey she was feeling compelled to take. She had accomplished so much during the course of her life, but still her body believed she would be punished for following her dreams. She experienced that punishment every day in vague forms that frustrated her mind.

During one particularly enlightening session, her therapist guided her into a light trance to explore another fragment of the Heart Child. A weight compressed Ellen's heart as she described how the child was confined in a cage, its nearly naked body slumped over in hopelessness and humiliation. A paralyzing numbness suddenly spread through Ellen's body, a feeling she had often known as a child. She was surprised this feeling had surfaced. Hadn't she moved past all those issues years ago?

Instinctively she shifted her attention to the sunshine filtering through the leaves outside the window, and let the fear sink back into the depths. She couldn't see herself as fearful and weak. Most of all, she couldn't let anyone else see her that way. It was too dangerous.

But the phantom child's deep anger pushed through her defenses, wanting to be acknowledged. In Ellen's life, anger had surfaced only as the resolve to carve an ambitious path in corporate politics. It helped her secure everything she had ever wanted. The child, increasingly agitated, suddenly threw itself against the bars of the cage, venting anger and grief with a vengefulness that frightened Ellen.

The bitter child symbolized an old pattern. Ellen had often protected herself from unfriendly forces behind a shield of angry defiance: "You can't hurt me no matter what you do."

It was a powerful weapon, personally and professionally, and she took satisfaction from the apparent control it gave her over others. Weakened now by cancer, Ellen no longer had the energy to support its presence in her body.

At last the child curled up on the floor of the cage to sleep and dream its angry dreams. She noticed the cage had no door, only the uninterrupted finality of cold steel bars. The child's fate was to die in its prison, alone, angry, unforgiving.

Ellen sobbed inconsolably at the utter desolation the child inspired in her. How could so much ugliness ever be repaired? This acknowledgment and acceptance was accompanied by a seismic restructuring that shook her body, breaking loose the pattern crippling her life.

"Do you know what this child is afraid of?" the therapist asked.

Ellen knew the answer. "The horrible anger in the people I grew up with. It felt like stones slamming into my heart." After a moment she said, "It makes me so sad."

"But the anger was theirs, wasn't it? Not the child's?" the therapist asked.

The question hung in Ellen's mind for a moment. In that space the gentle presence of truth entered, dissolving the burden of a lie that had long weighed on her life. "I can't believe how long I've thought it was something in me," Ellen said. "I felt so guilty."

"It's good to see the truth," the therapist said. "Now tell us what the child sees outside the cage."

"Some kind of monsters. I think the bars protect the child from attack."

Ellen never thought the emotions that haunted her could have shapes she could see. She was incredulous now that the ludicrous figures could have engendered so much fear. She watched as the bars of the cage melted away, freeing the child to enter a beautiful green world of sunlit meadows and peaceful skies.

Ellen was overcome with sadness. She had never grieved her life before. The therapist emphasized that Ellen was experiencing very old patterns that in no way reflected her true self. "Ellen, every moment you spend gaining knowledge of yourself moves you closer to health. Our work is just one way to create peace in your body. Follow the path your spirit offers, and you will find the life that is yours." Her words echoed the woman in Ellen's dream.

※

Into the Fire

A golden pond fills a corner of the field.
Stones of power send music from where they sit in the
sunlight – a crystal garden amidst the Arkansas hills.

As the disease eroded her vitality Ellen was often overwhelmed by exhaustion. In her entire life she had never felt so undone, so unavailable to herself. A kind of meltdown was undoing the very fabric of her being. She desperately wished to put everything on hold for a while, the cancer, the relationship, everything. She wanted to have control again, even if it meant saying no to the things that could save her life.

She called Daniel first thing in the morning. He answered the phone with his usual enthusiasm. "I'm just about packed and ready to go, my love. How are things on your end?"

Fear flooded Ellen as she tried to sound certain. "Daniel, I need to do this alone for a while. I don't want anyone here until I figure things out. I need to be by myself." The words sounded so final.

She felt him searching for a response in the long silence. "You know I love you, Ellen. I will always support you in whatever you feel is right, but how can it be right to go through this alone? I don't understand."

"Because I don't know what to do with love," she responded. "I don't know what it means to live, to love somebody and let them love me back. I feel more comfortable managing things on my own. Later on, when I know what's going to happen to me, maybe I can work on that, but right now I can't."

An awful silence followed. She felt beads of sweat on her forehead, but at the same time she felt the conflict that had been gathering in her heart finally resolve, releasing a flood of relief. The reins of control felt comfortable in her hands. Vulnerability vanished. She felt safe again.

Daniel accepted her position, but with great concern. "I know you can do this yourself. I never thought for a minute you couldn't. I had hoped to be with you because our life together would begin that much sooner. Has that become part of the question for you now?"

"My whole life is in question," she replied. "There's

nothing I'm sure about right now. And I don't have the energy to act as if I do. So I want to put what I can on the back burner for a while. Does that make sense to you?"

"Of course. I can't say that I've never had questions about my own life. What would you like me to do?"

"Just let me stop thinking about you for a while," she said. "I want to stop worrying about what's going to happen with us."

"I understand, Ellen. I'll let you work things through. Just know that I'm not going anywhere. And I want you to call when you can, to let me know how you're doing."

"That sounds fine," Ellen said. "I'll do that."

When she hung up, her world felt comfortable again. The chaos was pushed away, and she serenely made herself a cup of tea, enjoying the morning sun coming through her windows.

The next morning she prepared for her first chemotherapy appointment as if she were preparing for work. The doorman met her with a polite greeting as she stepped out to hail a taxi. She nodded, noting the surreal quality of the gulf that lay between them. His vital presence seemed so naturally connected to the life around them. She wondered what that must feel like.

The taxi dropped her off at the center where she would receive her treatments. Another world presented itself as she walked through the doors. The atmosphere overflowed with positive energy. She felt like a child in a place where children are welcome.

After the formalities of admission, she was shown into the infusion room. Creamy white leather recliners faced each other in two long rows. Patients sat with tall metal rollaway stands at their sides. Bags of medication hung on the stands. It dripped through tubes into the arms or chests of the patients.

Ellen chose a chair that gave her a view of the leafy courtyard. She watched the hot August sun filtering through the branches while a nurse deftly inserted a saline lock into a vein in her forearm. A subtle kind of fear took hold of her as the long transparent tube from the IV pump was attached. The experience was so alien. It felt to her like a distant dream.

The saline flush felt cool under her skin. The nurse then transferred the delivery over to the clear plastic bag holding the potent medication just delivered from the hospital pharmacy. As the chemicals entered her body and spread through her system, Ellen felt enlivened by a loving glow that brought relaxation and relief to her struggling spirit.

Forty-five minutes later she was checking out, elated by the unexpected strength she felt. She stepped into the world fortified by the positive support of people who had opened new doors for her in that unlikely place.

On the ride home she saw everything as if for the first time, the busy energy of the streets igniting the same excitement as when she had first arrived in Chicago. She never tired of passing through the traditional heart of the city, and seeing the beautiful monuments to commerce that somehow inspired a sense of romance and adventure.

She called Daniel to reassure him that everything was fine. Relieved to hear of her success, he wanted to celebrate by arranging a weekend cruise for her on Lake Michigan. She welcomed the idea, her fears dissolving in a rush of excitement.

The next morning she greeted the doorman with enthusiasm as he ushered her to a taxi. Surprisingly, she found the young driver interesting rather than disquieting, with his pierced eyebrows and aggressive manner. Her reaction was markedly different than what she expected. The emotions she traditionally used to protect herself in such circumstances were strangely subdued and empty. The young man was no longer a reflection of her fears. At some level she even felt a gentle kinship with him.

But on Wednesday, the gift of vision that had graced Ellen's being washed away like the tide, leaving her feeling flat and empty. Instead of buoying her up, Wednesday's treatment hurled her into an abyss of weariness and confusion. It was all she could do to get home and fall into bed.

In a dream she saw herself buried to the neck in quicksand, struggling to stay alive. She woke up and knew her spirit was trying to avoid being pulled under. Ellen used visualization to revisit her dream. Someone she could not see had laid planks across the quicksand. When she managed to reach solid ground, she found herself on a beautiful beach. A deep azure sea stretched to the horizon, and Ellen wondered how she could have thought the ocean was a pit of quicksand. But then she noticed that the muck from the bog still clung to her body. She wanted to wash off in the sea, but fear paralyzed her. She couldn't bring herself to move toward the beautiful blue waves. It was too much beauty, too much freedom for her to claim. The moment passed, and the fear remained in her heart.

As the reverie faded, Ellen was left with a realization: "The water of life will fill any vessel I pour it into. Life makes my patterns real. If they feel like a swamp, that will be my experience." She was amazed that so much time had passed in this tragic delusion. Exhaustion and relief swirled through her mind as she drifted peacefully to sleep.

Ellen's weekend cruise on Lake Michigan was spent mostly in her stateroom, sleeping. She woke for meals and short walks on deck, but her body demanded rest. The soothing presence of water made it easy to relax.

She called Daniel when she got home to let him know how much better she felt. He was delighted to hear from her. He said it seemed far too long since he'd seen her. But it would be several months more before they would meet again.

Coming to Terms

Two dogs nuzzle and lick as we sit on the ground, my spirit and I, looking for points of light in the red earth.

The patterns that had driven her career now propelled Ellen headlong into healing. While the doctors attended to her body, Ellen continued her exploration of the deeper, hidden elements of her inner world. She discovered a traditional Korean bathhouse where a community of women, mostly Koreans, moved through the rituals of personal care with a sense of entitlement that intimidated Ellen at first.

Several times a week she entered the simple reception area, where she was given a light robe and two towels folded neatly around one another. Leaving her shoes in the anteroom, she removed her clothing and entered the bathing area naked, going first to a long bench where she took a seated shower. Next she soaked her feet in a wooden bucket filled with herbal water, and scrubbed her skin with loofah cloths. Finally she sat in several pools of varying temperatures, enjoying the mineral rich waters.

Large rooms dedicated to various healing modalities surrounded the bathing area. Ellen entered the salt room first. A thick layer of warm sea salt crunched beneath the canvas covering on the floor. A pleasant heat saturated her body as she found a comfortable position. Her head rested on a pink satin pillow.

The heated salt pulled impurities from Ellen's body. After the salt experience, the sand room comforted her body like lying on a warm beach. Finally Ellen entered the jade room and lay on grass mats floating on a bed of heated mud, bringing her energies into harmony with the earth's strength. Jade stones jutting from masonry walls washed her with blessings of love and abundance, gifts she had not given herself in a long time.

Thoroughly saturated with heat, Ellen bathed again in the pools and fountains of the spa. A body scrub from head to toe readied her for a nourishing massage. The massage therapist was also an acupuncturist whose training in traditional Chinese medicine gave Ellen another avenue of healing.

The massage therapist focused on clearing the gall bladder meridian that connected Ellen to her anger. Learning how the meridians channeled light through her body inspired Ellen to learn more about Chinese medicine. Over time Ellen came to understand that the therapies she discovered overlapped and complemented one another.

The steady infusion of chemicals into her body created unrelenting fatigue. Her life narrowed increasingly to allow only the activities that would contribute to her healing. Gradually she melted into the world around her. The energy it took to remain separate was dying.

As Ellen dismantled unhealthy ego patterns, her therapist suggested she give her ego a name. She named it Bob, and gradually recognized the unreasonable nature of the demands and complaints it pursued her with. Ellen's disease was stripping away the energy her ego thrived on, giving her the opportunity to clearly see the patterns that supported its reality. The therapist asked her to list all the people, places, and things that had caused her to be frightened or angry, beginning as early as she could remember.

In the weeks that followed, Ellen made other lists like the first, each defining a part of her ego's old character. She saw the fear she'd held so long, examined how it came to be and how it affected her. She claimed her pain instead of feeling guilty about her experiences and choices in life.

Her therapist gave Ellen seven areas to examine in relation to each person, place, or thing on the first list: pride, personal relations, sex life, self-esteem, security, finances, and ambition. As Ellen identified her old uses of energy, she saw things she could change that would bring her life more in balance with her growing spiritual awareness. Struggling to accept the way she had been treating herself, to stand in the center of her own experience no matter how unsettling, empowered Ellen to feel hopeful about her ability to create happiness in her life. She was clearing space inside herself for the harmonious elements of her spirit to reside.

As Ellen took her experiences apart, she looked not only at what had happened to her, but also at her own contribution to the pain in her life. It was difficult for her to accept the responsibility for the harm she had perpetrated against herself and others. Facing her shortcomings felt like rubbing salt into an open wound, but through this process Ellen's rational mind began to understand the burdens she carried. Sometimes it required several days to process these new thoughts, but as she did, Ellen began to experience a more joyful and spacious relationship with life. She was discovering how to be vulnerable without being fearful.

At the top of her resentment list was Daniel's name. It was as if she held him responsible for every awful thing that had ever happened. After his name she wrote pages overflowing with pain and loss. Bitter tears streamed down as she read the words to herself. His abandonment seemed unforgivable.

Weeks later she found a way to accept her pain. She was in the jade room lying on the warm mats, dozing in the comfortable silence. In a dream she saw a babe, serene and fat, lying naked on the verdant ground, awash in the calm twilight of evening. Ellen knew the babe was herself. A strong brown woman lifted the babe from the ground, deftly tying the child on her back with a soft woven cloth. The babe lay secure against her strong body as the magnificent woman moved confidently through the red desert night. Her steps never faltered. Her direction was sure. The babe felt known and loved by the woman. The Earth Mother carried the child where she could not go by herself, across the dark abyss of change.

After the vision passed, Ellen heard the Earth Mother tell her to take strength from the earth and let it heal her body. She spoke about how good it was to live a life with play and pleasure in it. She told Ellen that sadness and hopelessness could not make the foundation of a good life.

Floating on the warm mud, Ellen asked the Earth Mother to teach her songs of love so she could learn to sing them to herself, and learn to walk through the world supported by health and true abundance.

When she returned to her writing that day, Ellen was finally ready to examine her own part in her relationship with Daniel. Searching for the truth that lay beneath the years of loss, Ellen considered how she had been selfish, how she had used the relationship for her own gain. In retrospect she saw that she had needed the relationship to feel good about herself. Being in love kept her from drowning in her own difficult life.

She realized she had never told Daniel how desperately she wanted out of her life back then. She pretended she was on top of things, and whatever he did was fine with her. She saw the pain she had caused him by her sudden loss of commitment to their plans. Ellen realized she had wanted their relationship to fix everything she didn't feel good about. She needed Daniel to make her feel wanted and loved, when she did not feel that way toward herself.

Ellen remembered being afraid she would die if she had to face life alone. She realized those fears had driven her experience in other ways, too. Her fear of death had become the fear of losing what she had, even though she had diversified her acquisitions long ago to guard against that possibility.

Lastly, she asked herself whom she had harmed and how had she harmed them. She already knew of the harm she had brought to herself by holding so much grief and anger through the years. Now she saw how much she had hurt Daniel. When they had parted so long ago he carried an innocent trust that life would be good for them. He still seemed to live in that place of innocent trust. Or perhaps she just wasn't aware of the pain that might still cling to his life.

Letting Go of Darkness

Holding On to Normal

The crystal man sits across from us, his energies blending beautifully with this place.

Gradually the healing care Ellen was receiving began to help. As she searched for ways to heal her inner life, chemotherapy was doing its job of beating back the cancer. Halfway through her treatments, she began to experience a growing sense of vitality and a strong desire to get back to normal life.

With the trepidation of a schoolgirl, she called her boss and set up a meeting. Her four months away from work seemed like a lifetime. She was surprised when she entered the suite of offices that had once seemed so stifling; everything seemed brighter, more spacious than when she left. People greeted her with genuine gladness, many exclaiming how well she looked. Her boss was happy she was ready to return to work.

After the meeting, she stopped for lunch in one of the cafes she had passed so many times in the old days. Today life felt peaceful, smooth, unfurled. The people sitting nearby felt like warm, familiar friends.

When she told Daniel she was returning to work,

he was hesitant to give his blessing, but her insistent optimism convinced him to embrace her choice. Confident elation followed her through the next weeks as she renewed her commitment to the life she had put aside. Easily connecting to her familiar routines, Ellen discovered energy and enthusiasm she hadn't felt in years. The suffocating feeling was gone. She eagerly took on more responsibility than anyone thought she should, so intent was she on proving that all was well.

As the month passed Ellen prepared for her next chemotherapy week by maintaining her macrobiotic diet and spending enough time out of doors to keep her energy well supplied.

Even with this preparation, the fourth round of chemo hit her hard. Previously she had been able to push away the effects with a weekend of solid sleep, but this time the chemicals washed through her brain and the residue didn't go away. The nurses had mentioned people getting "chemo brain," but until now Ellen hadn't known what they were referring to.

The caustic effect made it impossible to connect to life in the outside world. The energies that connected her to reality felt blown to bits.

A friend offered the use of a machine he used

training for triathlons, and it saved her from a complete meltdown. Using it after having chemotherapy was like waking up from a bad dream. The natural currents that streamed into her hands and feet from the machine revived her mind and rejuvenated her body.

The twenty-minute treatment lifted her out of the disabling fog. Ellen used the machine twice more the first week after chemo. Her determination to get life back to normal was being aided in unusual ways.

Her naturopathic doctor monitored the lab work from the cancer center in preparation for each new treatment. He noticed her body was not absorbing the B vitamins she was taking and recommended weekly injections to handle the faulty absorption.

Ellen noticed a difference immediately. She felt solid in mind and body, and more at ease. It was apparent that the deficiency had been a major factor in the deterioration of her immune system. After six weeks, Ellen was taught to inject the vitamins herself. It was no small matter. If the nurse hadn't been so patient, Ellen would never have been able to stick herself in the rear with the needle.

Ellen's acupuncturist, seeing that her digestive system was very weak, was stimulating meridian points to release energy blockages and bring all her organs into harmony with one another. After her first treatment, she woke in the middle of the night with a very agitated stomach. Something long closed was finally opening.

Her habit had been to slump over her stomach as if there were nothing there to hold her up. As she lay in bed, Ellen became aware of a terrible concentration of self-hatred that was beginning to move upward through her body. A series of pictures passed through her mind, the most shameful ones lingering in the darkness.

A wave of energy rose up through her chest and into her throat, stopping at her forehead. Ellen felt a dull pain. She was resisting letting go of something, but she couldn't figure out what. When she asked inside what the lesson was, she heard clearly that it was to see things joyfully, to appreciate herself and life. It occurred to Ellen that her disease wasn't cancer—it was self-hatred. Its dark presence in her body became less distinct as she drifted back to sleep.

Ellen's dreams continued to be vivid reminders that change was indeed upon her, even if her efforts were focused on keeping her old life essentially intact. One dream in particular stuck with her. She was in a speeding car, flying up a mountain so fast the landscape was a blur, unable to slow it down even as the summit came into view. The car flew over the crest into empty air. She clung to the steering wheel as the car plummeted thousands of feet. She knew she would die if she stayed in the car.

Below her Ellen could see the shore of a great ocean. "If I can dive into the ocean, I'll be safe." That thought compelled her to action. Climbing out of the falling car and using the air currents to guide her body, she dived gracefully into the turquoise waves. She found herself in an oddly familiar community of people; family and friends enjoying themselves in a beautiful sunlit realm under the sea, happy and safe.

Daniel, hearing about the dream, said it sounded like the ocean was calling her. It seemed a long while away, but she promised to visit him in California when her treatments were done. The decision felt good. The trip would be something to look forward to after chemotherapy.

A Spiritual Path to Wellness

Finding Her Light

*His peaceful voice is a path of light that takes me
from where I've been to where I want to be.*

It was becoming more and more difficult to endure each week of treatments. Just as she felt she was beginning to repair, it was time to start again. In her fifth month the unthinkable happened. She was waiting for an elevator when she felt herself begin to black out. As her mind reeled, she frantically looked for something to hang on to. Before she collapsed she saw someone calling for help on a cell phone.

She woke up in a hospital bed, unable to move or feel her body. Leaden heaviness bloated every cell. The wail of a siren from the street below triggered a storm of panic. She had no energy to push away the fear. The siren made real the omnipresent brutality that would kill her if she became the focus of it. Every situation, no matter how mundane, contained potential threats to her survival. She could do nothing except fall into the black hole of fear that threatened in the darkness of her mind. The inevitability of it suddenly sobered her and she entered the void ready for the death she knew was there. She was surprised by the potent stillness that surrounded her, instead of the chaos she had expected. The stillness nourished her. There was no substance to the fear she had carried so long. It could die with the ghost that created it.

Tests couldn't reveal the cause of her collapse. As the paralysis began to fade, a nurse helped her eat applesauce and drink juice through a straw. Ellen was glad for the woman's company. A full moon arced across her window. The nurse softened the lights as she left Ellen to sleep. The soft night sounds of the hospital surrounded her as she drifted into a dream.

Ellen found herself in a beautiful department store. The atmosphere was serene as she prepared to open the store for morning shoppers. She was the manager, efficient and well dressed. As she spoke with a coworker, a lovely young woman and her daughter walked up to the counter. The pair's couturier clothing and fine makeup accentuated their great beauty. The daughter smiled grandly as the mother asked Ellen to give her nine cents.

A pile of coins was on the counter, and Ellen motioned for the woman to take the money from there, watching as the woman took considerably more than nine cents. Ellen became indignant, angrily demanding that the woman give back the extra money along with a medallion that everyone called "the gold coin."

Writing of her dream later, Ellen wondered if she wasn't witnessing a familiar victim role, in which she routinely inflated the particulars of a situation to bring more importance to the issue and to herself for making things right.

In the dream the woman gave back some of the coins, but not everything. The woman moved behind the counter, closer to Ellen. In a rage Ellen struck her, knocking her to the floor. The woman did nothing to defend herself, denying that she owed Ellen more. Sitting on the woman's back, Ellen reached for a heavy vase and slammed it into the back of the woman's head. She heard a thud as the woman's forehead slammed against the marble floor. Ellen knew the grave harm she had done, but did not allow the knowledge to enter her heart.

Waking from her dream, Ellen realized she had been thinking that something had been taken from her which she was not prepared to give, even though the pile of coins sat carelessly on the counter. Her attention was on the organization of her life, not on developing the golden qualities of her spiritual nature. It was as if life came to ask for something back, something that Ellen had been given but had paid little attention to. Still, she didn't want to give it up. She felt it was hers, whether she valued it or not.

She felt the ancient and oppressive slab of anger press her heart and lungs, numbing her body. It was a cold emptiness that had persisted through the years. She had often tried to understand it but this was the closest she had ever come to experiencing its raw presence. Ellen wondered if this was a part of herself that couldn't be removed. She considered the hopelessness of a life where she couldn't get away from it. She didn't have the energy anymore to keep looking for things that would distract her from its life-killing presence.

In the soft hum of the hospital room, Ellen asked her angels to take this anger from her, but it remained. In desperation she asked the angels to help her see into its darkness, to find its meaning. Suddenly the hard shell of fear around her body exploded and a brilliant light burst free. She rested in its beauty and peace, knowing that the work of breaking out of the ego's realm of blindness and limitation was now complete.

Ellen understood that in her dream she had been the ego, an arrogant perfectionist, belligerent and demanding. The ego was unable to recognize the woman and her child as the harbingers of a new life. The woman, as a personification of Ellen's spiritual intelligence, wanted Ellen to recognize the golden part of herself, something the unenlightened ego had set aside.

But in the dream Ellen's ego chose against generosity, attempting instead to kill the intelligence that could save her. The ego saw spirit as threatening its own survival and sought to destroy the rebirth in Ellen's life. But nine is the number of completion; it signifies the transformation of the past into a new cycle of expression. Despite the ego's violent resistance, a new birth was imminent. The blaze of light that lit every cell of her being showed Ellen the truth about herself. She no longer believed the fear that had imprisoned her for so long. Now she could begin to understand love.

Daniel came to her room the next morning, flowers spilling from his arms. "I didn't know what to bring you," he said, laying the bouquets at the foot of her bed. Ellen burst into tears.

"Here." He gave her a handful of tissues, wrapping an arm around her shoulders. "I have a feeling everything's going to be just fine. I didn't know what to expect when I got here, but you look radiant. Tell me how you feel," he said, twining his fingers with hers.

"Undone, obviously," she replied, smiling. "I really thought I could do this by myself. I just didn't know how discombobulating it would get."

"There you go, using those big words again," he teased. "How about getting you home to your own bed? We have a taxi waiting for us downstairs."

They were in the lobby, flowers and all, before the nurse had Ellen's discharge papers ready. Daniel tucked the folder of doctor's instructions under his arm. Ellen was relieved to have him with her. A channel had opened that finally allowed her to be what she was, a person in need of help at a time of need. She didn't even feel guilty. It was what it was.

"I'm glad you're here," she said as the taxi sailed through the blustery streets. "In the past I always pushed away things I really needed. Now I trust what's in front of me." Ellen was beginning to understand how Daniel contributed to her well-being, and she to his. Their spirits were at ease together. Difficult things weren't so hard when their spirits were in harmony.

Lifting the Veil

*In the crystal garden we find the light I knew our
journey would bring us to. A tender gratitude sweetens
my heart, as the sacred stones vibrate in the sun.*

Not long after her hospital stay, Ellen discovered another piece of the puzzle. The neurologist ordered three tests to shed light on her blackout. One was a sleep test that required an overnight stay in the sleep center.

Checking in at seven o'clock, Ellen was shown to a private room where a technician patched numerous wires to her body. As she slept, the wires sent information to a monitor down the hall. Periodically a person reading the results came back to check or adjust the wires.

Surprisingly, she slept very well. At about one a.m. the technician brought Ellen a breathing device, saying her tests showed she had severe sleep apnea. The part of her brain that regulated breathing didn't operate normally when she slept, preventing her from entering the deepest stage of sleep where the body maintains and repairs itself. He explained that as she moved into deep sleep, her body quit breathing. With oxygen levels dropping, she constantly had to wake herself for air. Only in the deepest realms of sleep can the immune system fully repair the day's damage to the body, and Ellen never slept that deeply. The lack of oxygen through the night caused her to wake up groggy. The machine should enable her to receive oxygen throughout the night to correct the problem.

The technician woke her the next morning, asking how she felt using the device. Ellen said she'd rarely felt so clear and rested. But she was shocked to learn that she had apnea. She didn't snore, and she wasn't overweight. The neurologist made it clear that those things contribute to apnea, but the main part of her problem was in the brain center controlling her breathing.

Ellen was finding many tools to help her with the puzzle of her health. The breathing device. The juicer. The B injections. Giving up sugar. Sometimes she simply allowed herself to cry at the difficulty of making so many changes. Life suddenly seemed to require so much attention.

Ellen's chiropractor continued to help open her energy channels. When he adjusted her body, a cloud of heavy fatigue would spill out, released from deep wells of darkness finally opening to the light.

Ellen envisioned a runner in her pattern of fatigue: a man who never stopped moving. If he wasn't running somewhere, he was running in place. He never seemed to tire. She saw that he was always running to make things right. It was a kind of race she was in with those who would point out things that needed fixing. If she fixed them fast enough and well enough, then nothing could ever go wrong. It was her way of avoiding the confrontation and criticism she always expected from people.

Given the unyielding nature of the pattern, Ellen sought help from several disciplines she had not already tested. She established a healing day for herself. She chose Tuesday and made appointments with both a hypnotherapist and a life coach on the same day.

Ellen arrived not knowing what to expect. She saw the life coach first. He asked her if she had any specific goals to accomplish in their session. She indicated the places on her neck and head where the energy remained stuck, despite all the work to get it moving. She described the unusual pattern that controlled that area. No shadow children lived there. The runner was always dressed in an athlete's outfit, and he had a well-defined body, very muscular. But he had the same empty eyes as the beautiful shadow child. No communication reached him, so compulsive about his activities was he. His life was completely cut off from Ellen's.

"A woman has an inner partner that is a man, just as a man has an inner companion that is a woman," the life coach said. "It is part of who we are. The inner partner holds the key to becoming all we are capable of. This partner can bring terrible ruin if its potential is not discovered and given reality. But through love and art it can light the way into the dark realms of the inner world, that we may return whole. It mediates between the ego and the light, and is a great power in life."

"I don't see this man as anything but a slave driver," Ellen said.

"He is driven by fear. He works only to keep his world safe. In that world the masculine qualities of initiative and courage have become hard and cold. You have never questioned his power over your life. His compulsion is wholly bound to your ego's needs."

"How can I transform his power into a positive element of my life?" Ellen asked.

"By finding the courage to explore the fear that negates his higher expression in your life. Our inner partners grow as we do. Yours has bound itself to the physical world because it survives best there. It is capable of bringing so much more love and meaning into your life. Its great powers of transformation and transcendence have gone unused, unexplored, because of your fear. We can follow that fear back to the beginning and see its genesis if you'd like."

Ellen relaxed in the pillows of the couch as the life coach asked her to close her eyes and visualize a sanctuary where nothing but good could happen. Ellen saw herself as a small child, the Heart Child. She was in a clearing surrounded by beautiful redwoods. Filtered light softly warmed the ground. Her spiritual family was gathered around her.

The life coach asked her to look for a tunnel nearby. Searching with her family, she found a tunnel that appeared to go into a rock outcropping. The coach asked her to enter the tunnel and move toward a light at the other end. Ellen's Guardian of Wisdom entered the tunnel with her. Something appeared from the darkness to block the way, but her Guardian cast it aside. She saw the light at last and stepped out into it. It was blinding at first, but she soon saw that she was standing on top of a grassy hill. The coach asked her to look at her skin. Her arms were a deep olive-brown color. "What do your shoes look like?" he asked. Ellen saw rough leather sandals on her feet, and realized she was a boy, perhaps fourteen or fifteen.

"What year is it?" the coach asked.

"Eleven hundred something," the boy answered.

"Where are you?"

"Lebanon."

"Is anyone with you?"

The boy looked around. "No. But there are sheep, about thirty of them. I'm a shepherd," he said, a note of surprise in his voice.

"What time of day is it?"

"Near sunset, time to go home. I can see the town where I live across the valley."

"When you get there, where do you go?"

"To the low house where I live."

"Do you know anyone nearby?"

"My sister lives across the way. I help her with her family. She has two boys she raises by herself. Her husband died of disease when the children were small."

"Do you live alone?"

"Yes."

"Has it always been that way?"

"Since my sister married I have lived alone."

"Is this sister someone who is in your life now?"

"Yes. They are all in my life now."

"What happened in that life?"

"When we were small, my sister and I lived with our parents. I was frightened of the violence between them. Our life was often chaotic. I was afraid to sleep in the house at night, so after dark I would sneak out and look for things I could defend myself with. I hid the weapons in my bed.

"Then when I was eight or nine, my grandfather died. We set out to my uncle's village so my parents could get the inheritance money. We walked for several days before my parents started fighting. My mother was trying to defend herself from my father's blows. I pulled a blade from its hiding place in my clothing and stabbed him. As he was struggling with his wounds, my mother began hitting me, and I stabbed her. My sister was horrified as we watched them bleed to death on the dusty road. She helped me bury them under piles of rocks."

"What happened then?"

"We continued to my uncle's, telling him our parents had sent us to get the money. He gave it to us and we returned home, telling our neighbors that our parents had to stay with our uncle to help with family business. My sister married a very kind man several years later, and began to be happy when her boys were born. It looks like I carry the guilt of that day to the end of my life."

"Has it followed you into this life?" the coach asked.

"Exactly. My Spiritual Guardian tells me that this life can be the end of that cycle. I can use this lifetime to restore normal relations with my parents and get rid of the anger I have toward them. I never supposed it was my own hand that set such a negative cycle in motion. That's a shock."

"Yes," the coach said. "Things are often not as we might assume. And nine hundred years, more or less, is a long time to suffer such a burden.

"Now," he continued, "we're going to come back through the tunnel of time to your sanctuary. Do you see a light?"

"Yes. My Guardian is taking me toward it."

"Good. Tell me when you've arrived in your sanctuary."

"We're going slowly so I can look at all the beautiful crystals in the rock. I didn't see them before."

"When you arrive back, just take your time. Rest a bit. Absorb the experience. Then we'll come back here."

Ellen opened her eyes and saw her coach smiling at her. "That was amazing," she said. "Everything felt so real. Coming back, I felt like a different person. It was a terrible thing, but now that I understand what happened I feel ready to move forward."

"Your inner partner will only lose his compulsive fearfulness over time, but it will happen. Your job is to remain willing to question those compulsive fears that do not serve your spirit's well-being. As the light in you continues to inform your decisions, the old traps and obstructions will fall away. There is nothing real to hold them in your life; only what you thought was real."

Home

*I feel a beauty in my spirit I thought could never be.
At last I am home.*

When Ellen went to her appointment with the hypnotherapist, energy flowed freely through her body. The blocks were finally gone. She felt comfortable and at ease, so nothing urgent came up when the therapist asked what the purpose of their session was. Ellen mentioned the medical treatment she was having. The hypnotherapist asked if she would like to meet her inner physician, and Ellen agreed immediately.

The therapist asked Ellen to lie back and relax as she was guided through a journey connecting her to the energies at the earth's center. Then as she counted slowly to five, Ellen went ever more deeply into the center of her own spiritual world where what she needed would be given freely.

"What do you see around you?" the therapist asked.

"I am with my spiritual family again, but we are home," Ellen said.

"Describe your home to me."

"It is a beautiful land full of light. A great mountain stands to the North. My Guardian of Wisdom lives there. The castle in the East is where my Mother lives. My Father lives in the castle that stands in the West. A great courtyard joins the two where they are together most of the time. My Heart Child plays in the streams and forests of the South. I am the light that lives at the center. I feel very loved here."

"Join your Mother and Father in the courtyard for a while," the therapist said. "Your inner physician will come to you there." Ellen's body in the land of light was perfect. She was a young woman clothed in a simple brocade dress that touched the toes of her slippers. Mother pointed to the approaching figure of an old man, bent with age. As he came closer, Ellen recognized him. It was Dr. Bordeaux, the doctor who had delivered her and treated all her childhood ills. His presence was magic. Whatever her ailments, they disappeared almost as soon as she saw him.

As he joined them, it was apparent he was very exhausted. He sat with them at the table in the courtyard. "The worst is over," he said softly. Ellen knew he was talking about her illness. Father took the doctor's arm and assisted him inside for refreshment and rest. He had worked so hard for Ellen that his own resources had been severely taxed. She was grateful for his appearance in her life again, and thrilled that he was her inner physician.

Before she left, Mother and Father brought her something whose beautiful brilliance shone from their hands. It appeared to be a large crystal in the shape of two pyramids fitted together at their bases. It emanated a powerful force of light and energy. She held her hands out to receive it, but her parents moved past her hands and set it inside her heart. Love shone from their faces.

When it was time to return to the confines of the therapist's office, Ellen was reluctant to do so. But when the counting was complete, she opened her eyes and was back. The visit to her spiritual home had given her increased energy. She remembered seeing something there she hadn't seen before.

"What was it?" the therapist asked.

"It was like a pet, a little hairless monkey. It really liked my Father. It climbed on his shoulders and played with everyone. But when the Heart Child came to visit, the monkey stayed with her."

"Perhaps it is the Heart Child's shadow," she said. "Its playfulness points to the growth and freedom you have brought into your life. When the shadow is accepted for what it is, there is no longer anything to fear. We can relax and enjoy what is around us."

"I can feel that happening" Ellen said. "Is there anything else I can do to help myself get better?" she asked.

"A number of my patients create visualization treatments they use on themselves every day. Let your spirit play around with that for a while and see what develops. The visualization you choose should be exciting to the part of you that likes to have fun."

Over the next few days Ellen remembered the Pacman games she liked to indulge in when she was in college. She visualized a multitude of the little gobbling heads going through her body devouring the cancer cells that had no chance against them.

Each night before going to sleep she watched as her body was swept clean of disease by the friendly marauders. Friendly to her, anyway. The nightly ritual brought more peace to her sleep.

Ellen continued her journey toward healing until finally the end was in sight. The chemo treatments had taken her to her limit. When the nurse took the lock from her vein for the last time, Ellen felt a glow in her spirit. It was over. She had done it.

Her journey made her stronger, more resilient, more loving. Before, she had persevered only to get through to some other place. Now life felt like hers. Ellen had returned to the path of the Heart Child. She no longer struggled. Life was embracing her with open arms.

When Ellen first entered the cancer center, she had been unprepared for the love and joy she received there. It took her a while to realize that the world outside was light years behind in the science of love. She saw miracles daily because an abundance of love and light were consciously and continually channeled into the environment. Everyone there reminded her that love heals, something she had lost touch with long ago.

Leaving the treatment center on the final day, Ellen was surprised to feel sad. "What is it?" Daniel asked, as they walked to their favorite place for lunch. The midwinter day was unseasonably warm. "In an odd kind of way, I'm going to miss that place," Ellen said. "There was so much positive energy there. I'll have to find other places where people are so positive."

"Unless you're on vacation, those places can be hard to find," Daniel said. "But we'll search them out."

After their celebration trip to California, Ellen returned to work, but the life she wanted was on the Coast. After a year tying up loose ends and receiving positive results from her cancer checkups, she moved to San Diego and took a position in Daniel's yacht brokerage firm, overseeing financial affairs.

In San Diego she found a personal trainer, a simple step that had a positive impact. When Ellen first started working out, her trainer talked about isolating the muscle groups to increase the efficiency of her effort. She couldn't understand what he meant because her whole body was habitually tense. About three months into the training, when her muscle fibers began responding individually to the various demands the weights placed on them, she finally realized how tightly she'd been holding everything. She was doing knee bends when she realized that the hard grip that held the weights in her hands was unnecessary. It took energy from the muscles in her legs that were doing the work.

As she continued the training her body began to remember its true form, and her shape changed to a younger, more athletic profile. Her functional strength increased tremendously, the kind of strength that gave her good sea legs.

Two years after cancer had turned her life upside down, Ellen was living a dream she would never have imagined possible. The shadow of disease still had a presence in her life, reminding her there are never any guarantees. But each day that she found herself alive was a day to celebrate.

One night when she and Daniel were sitting on their boat admiring the brilliant display of starlight dancing across the sea, Ellen said she'd like to adopt a child, one they could teach to love the sea in all its many guises.

"A latter-day Viking," Daniel said. "You know, there's something about the sea . . . when you're on it you're free. It would take a very special child to embrace this kind of life."

Later that night in the cabin below, Ellen dreamed of the child. She was strong and happy, walking through a beautiful green field awash in sunlight on her way to school. Her classroom was in the second story of a building overlooking a road lined with stately bungalows in a lush tropical landscape. A baby tiger ran playfully beside the child. It disappeared into the jungle as she climbed the steps to her classroom.

There were no students in the room, but the teacher had filled a number of water glasses with flowers. The child knew she had not come to attend class but to finish some work she had started.

Another person was there, someone the child knew but was surprised to see. This tall young woman was looking at a messy pile of boxes overflowing with stacks of papers that needed clearing. Before beginning the task, the child stood in front of the window admiring the lush landscape. A magnificent tiger was strolling up the other side of the road, strong and powerful. She watched intently as it passed, awed by its beauty.

In the moment it felt completely natural that a tiger should be strolling through the neighborhood. But after it passed, the child wondered if she shouldn't become alarmed. Because it seemed the normal thing to do, she asked her friend to call the police. When she did, there was a recorded message saying that so many people had called that the police were looking for the tiger to kill it.

The child looked out the window again, but saw

only the quiet neighborhood. The alarm seemed to be taking place only on the phone lines. Suddenly she saw the powerful animal striding up the hill, disappearing into the jungle. It emerged near a majestic tree that overspread the brow of the hill and climbed effortlessly into the towering foliage, stretching its massive body comfortably on a wide branch. There it resided, serenely confident in the power and beauty it possessed.

The child made her way to the towering tree and climbed up, finding a place to sit next to the tiger. She felt its powerful strength as if it were her own. The child realized that the tiger's life, strength, and power came from the tree. Her life came from it, too. The tiger had brought her here, that she might know.

"It will be a very special child," Ellen said as Daniel opened his eyes the next morning.

"Yes, I know. I dreamed of her, too."

Afterword

That we can touch the reality of our body's spirit with our physical senses and discover its immediate relationship to the life we are giving it, is something of which many of us may be unaware. The ability to perceive finer, more subtle matter than what we see or touch with our five basic senses is inherent in us all. This capacity for immediate spiritual perception gives us the information we need to raise ourselves out of conflict and need. As we create a personal vision to channel our spiritual energy, we are doing what is most natural as sons and daughters of an intelligent universe.

Supporting this process increases the well-being of all. Service to others aligns us with the energy that supports life, and we become channels for its flow into the world. Giving to others in love opens the way for more bounty to enter our lives. It allows us to grow toward the happiness and freedom that is our birthright.

It's amazing how beautiful and complex each of us must be simply to exist in this world. Finding this beauty in ourselves allows us to recognize it in others. As we open ourselves to the magnificent light that exists both within and without, its nourishing presence creates through us the love and beauty we all need to flourish.

The transformation that expands our reality into the fifth dimension of light and love begins with giving up the secrets that imprison us in the past. Journeying through the devastation held in those secrets brings us to a wall. The land of our spirit lies beyond. As we pass into that land, our spiritual family becomes known to us. We knew them before, but they were exiled from that land, as were we.

As the light becomes willing to give up its dependence on the ego's patterns, the ego takes its rightful place in the family of spirit. As we become more aware of ourselves as light, we see our proper relationship to each aspect of spirit that supports our life. As the inner world becomes our true home, we begin to see the outer life through different eyes. A conscious relationship with our Alpha Spirit grows from this fresh dynamic. We learn to experience life in a fundamentally new way. The old limitations of our dependence on ego give way to a bold development of our own potential through our partnership with this powerful aspect of spiritual and material reality. The development of that partnership will be explored in the next book of this series, *Letting in the Light*.

A Promise to the Day

This day I give my life to peace and abundance. I am grateful for the golden promise of my own spirit. I freely inhabit each moment with serenity and grace. I give my body and spirit the care and appreciation they deserve. I gift others with understanding and compassion, allowing them to gather wisdom in their own way. I am grateful for the many beautiful beings that support my well-being in this world. To all those seen and unseen comforters, I give my deepest gratitude.

Acknowledgments

This book has always been such a collaborative project that I could never express enough appreciation to the many beautiful people who have helped bring it to birth. The incredible clients I was blessed to work with through the years taught me the process by which we become truly human. Making the journey with them allowed me to better understand the process when it became my time to let go of the limitations I measured myself by. The work was no less painful, but at least I knew what was happening.

My family, as always, never doubted my desire to create this experience, even though I doubted myself on many occasions. Holly, my daughter, and Bernie, my son, were instrumental in so many ways to the success of this undertaking. I am forever grateful to them for what they have brought to my life.

Peter, my husband and guardian angel, enthusiastically supported the project since it began five years ago.

My father, Prospector John, has been very interested in the work's progress from the beginning. His encouragement has been invaluable.

My mother, Frances, has been a loving presence throughout the changes I have gone through while writing this book.

My grandmother, Mary Thompson, an artist during her lifetime, continues to show me with her presence that everything is possible.

I also wish to thank my daughter-in-law, Jeanne, for her beautiful dreams and my son-in-law, Randy, for his inspired words. Both contributed to the integrity of the message. I feel blessed they have become part of our family.

My friend Nannette says poignant things all the time, some of which found their way into these pages.

My agent and coach, Mark Ortman, freely provided his expertise from the beginning. Without his valuable assistance, this book would never have been finished.

When it was finally time to prepare the manuscript for publishing, a number of friends pre-read the book and offered many valuable suggestions, among them Bob Stewart, Tim Meuret, Valerie Huddleston-Kohler, and George Kohler. All these people are highly motivated and successful manifesters. I feel honored by their contribution to my life.

After the pre-reading suggestions were integrated into the manuscript it went to the concept editor, Lorrie Harrison, a dynamic woman who is an author herself, and lives in the San Juan Islands of Washington State. She beautifully fine-tuned the material to make it reader friendly. I learned a lot about writing by working with her. The high polish on the words came from Valerie Ann Sensabaugh, the copy editor. I was very touched by the spirit of love that reflects in her work.

You don't really know how things will turn out until everything starts coming together at the end. I'd always had a vision for the book, but turning that vision into reality was for the most part a mystery to me. Enter Bob Lanphear, art director par excellence. His professional expertise and guidance make the book what I always imagined it could be. My beautiful friend Anahata Joy Katkin brought her incredible talent to the project by designing the cover of the book.

Both of these people, Bob and Anahata, have very successful businesses, Bob with Lanphear Design, and Anahata with PaPaYa! What they give to the world is very beautiful and loving.

The photographs that grace these pages of writing were taken by two very fine artists. Both live and work in Washington State. Lisa Cooper's current work may be viewed at www.LisaCooperPhotography.com. Joseph Rosanno, whose photographs have been likened to those of Ansel Adams, shows his work in galleries nationwide. He may be reached about his work at JR@RossanoStudio.com.

Fourth Step Guide

WHO or WHAT	The REASON, WHAT HAPPENED

Fourth Step Guide

AFFECTED MY (All that apply)	MY PART (All that apply)
Self-Esteem; Ambitions; Sex; Relationships; Security; Finances; Pride	Was I Selfish; Inconsiderate; Frightened; Dishonest; Self-Seeking?

Bibliography
Selected & Recommended

Bethards, Betty. *The Dream Book: Symbols for Self Understanding.* Petaluma, California: NewCentury Publishers, 2001.

Chetwynd, Tom. *Dictionary for Dreamers.* London: Granada Publishing Ltd., 1984.

Das, Ram. *Journey of Awakening: A Meditator's Guidebook.* New York: Bantam Books, 1990.

D'Adamo, Dr. Peter J., with Catherine Whitney. *Live Right 4 Your Type.* New York: G.P. Putnam's Sons, 2001.

Gutmans, June. *Kahuna La'au Lapa'au.* Aiea, Hawaii: Island Heritage Publishing, 1994.

Jung, Carl G., and M.-L. von Franz, Joseph L. Henderson, Jolande Jacobi, and Aniela Jaffé. *Man and His Symbols.* Garden City, New York: Doubleday & Company Inc., 1964.

Kabat-Zinn, Jon. *Wherever You Go There You Are: Mindfulness Meditation in Everyday Life.* New York: Hyperion, 1994.

Kushi, Michio, with Stephen Blauer. *The Macrobiotic Way: The Definitive Guide to Macrobiotic Living.* New York: Penguin Group (USA) Inc., 2004.

McQ., Joe. *The Steps We Took.* Little Rock, Arkansas: August House, Inc., 1990.

Mitchell, Stephen. *The Enlightened Mind: An Anthology of Sacred Prose.* New York: HarperCollins, 1991.

Thie, John F., D.C. *Touch for Health: A Practical Guide to Natural Health Using Acupuncture, Touch, and Massage to Improve Postural Balance and Reduce Physical and Mental Pain and Tension.* Marina del Rey, California: DeVorss & Company, 1979.

Weil, Andrew, M.D. *Spontaneous Healing.* New York: Fawcett Columbine, 1996.

Wright, Machaelle Small. *Perelandra Garden Workbook, Second Edition: A Complete Guide to Gardening with Nature Intelligences.* Warrenton, Virginia: Perelandra, Ltd., 1993.

Write down your inspirations, dreams & revelations…

Write down your inspirations, dreams & revelations…

Write down your inspirations, dreams & revelations…

Write down your inspirations, dreams & revelations…

Write down your inspirations, dreams & revelations…

Write down your inspirations, dreams & revelations…

Order Information

To order copies of *Letting Go of Darkness*,
please visit
www.crystalgardenpress.com
or mail inquiries to

Crystal Garden Press
PO Box 443
Arlington, WA 98223

Quantity discounts available for
gift or educational purposes.